T0149194

INVARIABLE SNOW FOR THE ESKIMO . . .

With Respect; Native Alaskans

B. JOHNNY WAY

authorHOUSE®

AuthorHouse™
1663 Liberty Drive
Bloomington, IN 47403
www.authorhouse.com
Phone: 1 (800) 839-8640

Published by AuthorHouse   10/14/2015

ISBN: 978-1-5049-5406-8 (sc)
ISBN: 978-1-5049-5405-1 (hc)
ISBN: 978-1-5049-5407-5 (e)

Library of Congress Control Number: 2015916303

Print information available on the last page.

Any people depicted in stock imagery provided by Thinkstock are models, and such images are being used for illustrative purposes only. Certain stock imagery © Thinkstock.

This book is printed on acid-free paper.

CONTENTS

PREFACE

It is the authors intent to point out the obvious fact that we are all continuously learning throughout our lives starting from birth and continuing on. We have all, at one time or another, made a comment to ourselves that we would never forget how it was, or what it was like during a certain period of our lives. The author attempts to bring to life, just how a youngster learns of all that is new around him. The young boy in this story quickly learns how to navigate life with help from his family and those around him while ultimately realizing that learning is a process, and an ongoing effort by which we all learn through many different means. The young boy in this story tells of learning while having fun doing so. The little boy tells this story while the author includes articulate words- designed to build the readers vocabulary- though these very same words used in this book might very well have been words used in front of him, though not understanding these words meaning due to his young age. The young boy realizes quickly that we can actually achieve much more than just the much welcomed gratitude from helping each other. Friendships last forever. The ripple effect that comes from helping each other out, even strangers goes much further than we my think or can even imagine. The ripple effect of helping out others is so powerful, that we many never realize how much a simple kind word or a helpful gesture to someone can make their day so much more than just another day. The young boy in this story learns the upsides to life, while learning that there are consequences as well as a downside as well. Life, he soon learns, has many challenges, and by helping others we can achieve many great things together. Making friends everywhere we travel. Making long term friends due to moving to a new location is both important and fun, being "I do" or "IDeA"people; Note that these two anagrams are this authors own design, giving an identifying moniker to identify those proud and brave people who have moved from their ancestral lands, or any other region, in order to live harmoniously in another region. These two anagrams stand for "Indigenous Divergent Outlanders as "I Do" people, and or "Indigenous Divergent Auslanders" which when pronounced is "Idea's."

Learning that when it comes to a healthy life, a healthy surrounding is paramount, and therefore we should surround ourselves with the proper positive "can do" attitude. Healthy life comes from a healthy lifestyle, so we should stand tall with lots of good helpful friends, which is to say, our family. The advantageous thing to do is to start everyday with a good healthy breakfast, to prepare ourselves for the day with our positive outlook. Like a healthy body, knowledge is very important and it comes from personal experiences and reading good books. Healthy lifestyles can be achieved with proper eating habits, whereas this information can also be found in reputable cook books, i.e. I do reference a cookbook on the reference page, which I highly recommend as a wonderful start to preparing a healthy breakfast, lunch, and dinner.

A quote from this cookbook, "No experience? No problem. Let's get cooking!"

INTRODUCTION

Every living thing, every experience has a beginning, just like a story. Personally, my beginning, my entrance into this world, was the same as everyone else's. Well, not exactly the same as most everyone else's. Nevertheless, I was born ...

HEY, WHAT'S GOING ON?
WHAT JUST HAPPENED?

On Monday, April 30, 1956, shortly after eleven at night, I successfully made my entrance into this world through a slightly awkward and dangerous birthing ordeal known as a breech birth. After my birth, both my mother and I, though slightly traumatized, rested and recovered rather well, without any further trouble for the remainder of my postnatal care. Ultimately, though there was no real consideration given at that time, though it turns out that I was the last child born into this family, headed by my father, Raymond, and my mother, Dorothy.

Barring my awkward entrance into this world—well, that and the fact that I was allergic to regular milk formula—my life would be considered rather routine and normal for the following four years. However, there was one more shocking occurrence I experienced during my birth that I should mention.

Only moments after my birth, I was suddenly overwhelmed by an outburst of uncontrollable angst. The ambient temperature in the delivery room was considerably cooler than what I had previously been accustomed to, and this could have been the original atrocity that caused my initial discomfort. However, I believe that the main reason for my outburst was because somebody in that delivery room got a little slaphappy with my butt. This someone, who I assume was nonaggressive for the most part, grabbed me, held me upside down by my legs, and slapped my butt cheeks like a standing ovation! At least that was what if felt like to me.

No doubt the thoughts running through my mind at that particular moment must have been, *What the ?!%!#/**! is going on here?* Of course, all this unnecessary behavior on my part subsided as soon as certain postpartum needs were met, and shortly thereafter I was quite pacified and looking forward to a nice long nap for some inexplicable reason.

Shortly after my birth, perhaps a day or so, the lead doctor at the hospital, who was also the presiding doctor during my delivery, gave both my mother and me a clean bill of health and released us. This good news meant that we would get to go home. My first chance to see where I'll be living. While we were at it, I was going to get to experience my first ride home. Another first for me was the ride home in the family car. Cruising down the road in the family car looking straight upward. Yes indeed, everything is looking up from my perspective! I mean, after all, most of my time so far had been spent lying on my back, from which position I could only look up, or from side to side. It was a work in progress.

Life itself was looking rather normal for me, as with any healthy infant of the same age. The first four years of my life were mostly focused on accepting the standard and normal routines of life.

Unknown to me then, I was to participate in and accomplish many adventurous activities, including becoming the first boy astronaut to land on the moon by the time I was six. I would experience the joys of slicing and gliding around on a huge sheet of ice atop a frozen Alaskan lake and would be intentionally hurled high into the air by total strangers with the help of a very large blanket, and I would witness firsthand the larger-than-life, scary-looking sea creatures from the icy-cold waters of the Gulf of Alaska!

By the time I was six years old, I would have many stories to tell of fishing for sockeye salmon in one of the many streams and rivers of Alaska with my very own homemade fishing pole, made from the wood of a kid's toy kite. I would also have many opportunities to successfully wave at and greet the real-life Santa Claus himself.

All these adventures and more would be my very own experiences, seen through the impressionable eyes of my youth. It may be hard to believe, but all of this and much more would become my adventures, all by the age of six.

THE LESSON EXPRESS

From the start of my life, both my mother and father tried their very best to impress upon me, and my older siblings as well, all of the important, the uncomplicated, and the not-so-important matters of life. The fundamentals of life as I would soon be facing. Both of my parents were adamant of this, and therefore were continuously reminding us kids of the everyday dos and don'ts. My mother was the best at this, as she was the most patient person. She didn't just tell us about something one day and not the next, but rather she often repeated these lessons seemingly on a daily regimen—several times each day even, once or twice every hour for the important issues. Well, maybe it wasn't once or twice an hour . . . and, maybe not that often, but it sure seemed like it to us. Both my parents were ready to help usher my two older brothers and myself toward a better understanding of how life works. Lessons like how those around us are just as important as we are, and that every person is entitled to achieve the most out of life free of prejudice. I believe that was the paramount lesson to-which was on their list of lessons to be learned and understood. Not just learned, but understood. I call fundamental absorption. I remember my parents as being subtle yet repetitive with their advice regarding on how to live a decent and good life. Mom would repeat these lessons so us kids would understand and not just learn by rote. This type of repetitive teaching certainly worked out for me.

AS I RECALL, TIME WAITS FOR NO ONE

The year 1960 would ultimately be an important year for me simply because that particular year was when I began forming my first long-term memories as a young child. These memories are the very same memories that have lasted me a lifetime, and to which I can recall to this day.

As I recall, I was about four years old when I first began to break free of that fuzzy, memory-lapsing existence every young child experiences and breaks free of in his or her own time. I believe this process—which truly begins prior to our actual births and the following lack of cognizance for several months—is very crucial for our young minds' development and the formation of our individual personalities.

This process usually precedes our ability to form more complex, long-term, cognitive memory recall. It's all part of the learning process. There are, of course, some people who have childhood memories dating from a much earlier age than it took me. Ive heard that some people have experiences several months earlier than the forty-eight months it took me, and there are other people who have no real memories of their childhoods until the age of five or even later. I have to say, my memories began to form just as soon as things began making sense to me.

Any memory I have from before this point can only be described as feelings, unexplained figurative images without narrative meaning, or images one sees through perhaps a screen door or a smudged window. I can see these images in my minds eye, but I can't describe what it is I was looking at. Yes, I was somewhere around the age of four years old by the time my literal thoughts began forming cohesive patterns. This I expect is when I began developing and storing long-term, lifetime memories to guide me through life.

Following my birth, I was brought directly from the hospital to my first home, which was on Harriet Avenue in Campbell, California. Our house on Harriet Avenue was located in an area that was, at that time, still regarded as an agronomic rural community. I would live in this home with my new family for the first four months of my new life. However, soon it was necessary for us to move to a new location. Our second home was perhaps only 20 miles from our previous home in distance, but this new home had more neighbors with homes sitting side by side. A little different style of living on Agate Drive in quaint Sunnyvale, then it was in rural Campbell.

From that August day in 1956 until early 1960, I lived a pretty normal life, during which time I tried my best to understand the simplest of childhood complexities. And then, somewhere around my fourth birthday, I began to change . . . just a little. It was during this subtle, barely noticeable change that I started to remember much more than my name, age, or basically how to properly go to the bathroom on my own.

Now I'm pretty sure this time frame is accurate because I have only one memory of my grandma Lu coming over to our house to visit us, and that visit was in the summer of 1960. And if memory serves me well, her visit turned out to be a rather short one. Honestly, that's how I remember it. My memory from that visit is still vivid in my mind's eye, but a little out of focus. What I do remember of that day is it being a warm summer day. It was warm enough for all of us to be hanging outside in the front yard when she rolled up to our house. I have this slightly out-of-focus, fuzzy visual memory of my grandma Lu walking side by side with my dad, and of course with me following right behind the two of them, passing alongside this little old dingy-colored car parked in our driveway as we meandered on up to the front door of our house. Funny thing about that car.

Just a quick little side note: For many years I was under the impression that the dingy old car was my grandma Lula's car and that she drove herself to our house that day. That's not the case here at all. I was under the wrong impression all that time. Isn't it funny how we can miss some of the simplest details of certain events that easily? Even funnier is that whenever I would recall this story to other family members in the know, not one of them could recall us ever owning a grey car, dingy colored or otherwise sitting in our driveway.

I can personally attest to how important it is, and how grateful I am for all my family photos, as well as for my family members themselves, as they help me recall certain events of the past with more accuracy. I find it helps to be accurate when telling a story, it turns out my grandmother never drove a car in her life—apparently not ever. It's funny that I never saw that car sitting there before or after my grandma Lu's visit that day. And even funnier is that there is no other explanation for this memory of mine. Come to think of it, I don't think it was a car. It probably wasn't even our driveway. Ain't that a hoot! Must have been the wrong driveway.

I remember visiting with my grandma Lu only that one summer day, making that visit with her my very first long-term memory. Sadly, my grandma Lula passed away later that summer, just a few months shy of her seventy-fourth birthday. Because I have just, that one memory of her, I can easily say that that is my earliest memory as a child.

My grandpa Otis passed away in 1930, so I guess it's fairly obvious and goes without saying that I never got the chance to meet him or for that matter, ever got any real decent chance to get to know my grandma Lu, and I'm pretty sure she would have had some really nice and interesting stories to tell.

Now back to my family tree.

Grandpa Otis was born in January 1869, making him fifty years older than my dad and eighty-seven years older than me. To provide some historical perspective, my grandpa Otis was born approximately four years after George Washington Carver, the world-renowned American scientist, botanist, educator, and inventor, to whom we as a society still enjoy to this day, the hard work of his many inventions that most had been derived from— the peanut— hence peanut butter. As yet another reference point, my Grandpa Otis was two years younger than Wilbur Wright and two years older than Orville Wright, the two brothers credited with the first recorded sustained flight of a fixed-wing aircraft at Kitty Hawk in the great state of North Carolina in 1903. Grandma Lu was born in October 1885, a mere sixteen and a half years younger than Grandpa Otis.

I have continuously marveled at and considered this extreme age difference between my grandparents and myself to be very unique. How many people have grandparents that are nearly a hundred years older than themselves? All the same, as time rolled on and I got older, I would come to realized that indeed there are many people and cultures around the world that consider this age span of seventy-one and eighty-seven years to be normal. Since this revelation, I have met several people who shared their own stories of similar much older family members with their very own travel experiences. However, though I share with others in a type of fraternity, I still remain quite impressed whenever I consider the fact that my grandpa Otis and grandma Lula lived in a time so long ago. Just to see how much has changed in the world since their youthful years. The time period my grandparents lived in was so different from the time period I was raised in and even that much more different from today. Time moves on, and some things automatically change.

Now my mother's father, Henry, known lovingly to us kids simply as Grandpa or sometimes Grandpa G, was born in 1902, and Arilla, my mothers mother, to whom we all referred to as Grandma or Grandma G, was born the following year in 1903. Both Grandpa and Grandma G were born within three days of each other in the same month of August. And though they were certainly much younger than my other grandparents, they were still born many years before I was. Do the math.

My dad, Raymond Newel, was born in September 1919 in the great state of Oklahoma, though he was raised primarily all his young life in the beautiful beach community of Santa Cruz, California. My mother, Dorothy Mae, was born in December 1926 in the generous and magnificently beautiful country of Canada, our great friends to the north.

SEPARATED BY TIME AND FUNCTION

My grandpa Otis was born in 1869 and died at the age of sixty-one, when my dad was just eleven years old. Of course my dad never really got the time to get to know his father very well in their short eleven years that they had together- minus those first 4 years of fuzzy thoughts- but in that short amount of time, one thing is for sure, my grandpa made sure my dad learned the importance of having good character.

Tintype still photos and a few stories are pretty much all I've had to go by in order to get to know my grandparents on my dad's side a little bit better. The pictures of them from back in the late nineteenth and early twentieth century certainly helps put a little self-explanatory narrative to their own wonderful and personal story.

When I look at those pictures of my grandparents, I still marvel at what it must have been like to deal with their everyday particulars with such antiquated living conditions, especially in comparison to modern-day living conditions. They were obviously happy of course, and that is what truly matters. Still though, the fact remains that we have come so very far in terms of modern-day amenities and attire.

I have to admit that my grandparents- back in their day- looked very cool and stylish in these parlor-pose tintypes they left us. Very dapper indeed. I take my hat off to them because most of their clothes were made of denim and wool and of course cotton, among other fancier cloth. Their clothes were practical, which translates to mean affordable and within their budget. Even still, they really did make those clothes work for them, and of course they chose to wear these clothes for both comfort and practicality, while looking fashionable came with the proper decent attitude.

I am most definitely separated from my grandparents by both time and function. I certainly do come from a family with some extreme age differences. Grandpa Otis was eighty-seven years older, Grandma Lu was seventy-one, Grandpa G was fifty-four, and Grandma G was fifty-three.

Going back further yet, my great-great-great- … this could take a while … great-grandfather George Way first came to the Americas back in 1650's. Of course that's another story altogether, and that story is somewhat hazier yet.

ANYBODY REALLY KNOW WHAT TIME IT IS ... ANYONE?

Fifty-plus years have passed since I was a young boy just beginning to start my own life, which, by the way, included the ever-so-obvious youthful sense of everything being a new experience. That is exactly what all newbies experience from birth. No exceptions, every single child goes through this learning process, which in truth, is a great deal of learning.

When it comes to the theory of time and motion, some people's first thought is that fifty years is a very long time ... and really there is no chance of arguing that point. No matter how a person perceives time, fifty years is still half a century, and that equates to a very long period of time. To me, 50 years does seem like both a long time passing and while seemingly being not too long ago. Many spectacular events have taken place in the span of the past fifty years, along with many wonderful societal changes, that are not just limited to changes in how we dress or what we eat, but also include how society itself has adapted and taken on the initiative to change for a better understanding.

I choose to believe that the passage of time should and always will be determined by a particular individual's perspective and involvement with their own times gone by. Better put, a person reaps what he or she sows. The more exciting and productive things a person experiences during his or her life, the better his or her stories will be as transcribed through his or her own memories, personal involvement, and personal investment into life itself.

Each individual's past has a great influence on his or her present and is highly instrumental in the molding of who that person is to become, from a child's point of view, clear through to the complete development into an adult.

Our brains are wired with the ability to recall past events, from our past like stretching time so-to-speak. It can be very helpful and highly informative to those around us as we go about sharing our stories with other people, and in doing this while sharing our knowledge at the same time. Memories keep time from escaping us completely and keep us close to the past, through the sharing of merely a slight recollection, that can develop into a simple quaint story, or one that can become monumental to those who like to hear of those events. As long as we are living and as long as there is someone to whom we can trust to recall the past events accurately for us, then fifty years really shouldn't seem that long ago.

To me, the passage of time is no more of a mystery than the recollection of a beautiful memory. Time waits for no one!

BACK THEN AND FROM THE BEGINNING

My first wake-up call occurred in 1960. I know this was the year of my first cognizant memories because of the vivid memory I have of meeting my grandma Lu for what I have always considered as the first and only time of hanging out with her, or at least trying my best to carry on a decent conversation. Obviously all this is something of a thought memory that's been lingering in my mind all these years. I have been told that it really wasn't the first and only time my grandma Lu and I got together like that and that apparently, she had been over to our house on several occasions, though I honestly only remember her coming to visit just that one time. Ain't it funny how our memories work?

Needless to say, I'm still able to visualize seeing her during that one visit. I can see her and my dad standing there in the driveway by this old dingy-gray car of ours. That particular memory has stayed planted in my mind like a well-preserved still photograph after all these years, probably because I look back and think about that moment from time to time, which only proves to instill the thought even deeper. It seems as though that memory won't go away either. It's just one of those visual thoughts that remains solid and intact, albeit with a slightly fuzzier image as time moves on.

My grandma Lu was a pretty cool lady … I guess. And she and I got along super … I suppose. Or at least this is what I've been told by older family members in the know. I really don't remember very much of grandma Lu other than those few thoughts of mine, and I certainly can't prove whether what I've been told is true or not. I just have to believe it's so. After all, these stories were told to me by people I completely trust, and trust is a very honorable virtue.

It only stands to reason that since I personally do not have much recall of interacting with my Grandma Lu, and therefore having formed no personal knowledge of either my grandma Lu or my grandpa Otis, since he passed away long before I was born, I am thus entrusting other family members to tell me truthful stories of not just my grandparents and of their personal observations and interactions, but rather that of other family members and of their great adventures as well.

It turns out that I've had to learn to rely on family members to tell me the honest truth about most everything that occurred prior to my full cognizance of those particulars. I can honestly attest to the reality that having a family with such large time gaps between generations has some interesting disadvantages as well as some very unique advantages.

One thing I can say about my grandma Lu with absolute certainty is that she was a tall woman, and though my grandmother was of French ancestry and born into a proud family originally from the beautiful country of France, she was born and raised in the great state of Nebraska.

My grandpa Otis's had ancestral roots coming from both the proud and mighty English and Scottish isles. My Grandpa G, similar to Grandpa Otis had a combination of two different ancestral lines as well, whereby his family genealogy being rooted in the beautiful and majestic countries of Germany and Switzerland. My grandma G's family, though residing in beautiful Canada, has her genealogy roots traced back to the beautiful and proud people of Great Britain.

Of course being told at a young age that your grandmother and grandfather were part this or part that truly means very little to the young and innocent. Some minds are just too young to comprehend what all that means. I was taught to be proud of my heritage, and I am.

I was also taught from a very young age to respect everyone else's heritage and culture as well. And to this day I do with the utmost conviction. That one particular lesson happens to be one of the most important of all lessons, and therefore has remained and been a significant part of my character ever since I first understood that respecting others is the proper and normal behavior. There is always much more to a concept than just understanding, as the concept needs to be fully embraced to understand. It became a part of my life and therefore it's natural for me to feel that compassion for every one—so much so that I never give it another thought to show anything but intentional respect to others.

I have befriended many people from several different cultures, some of whom are first-generation Americans who have only recently been living in my local community for a very short period of time. Long ago I discovered it is easier to befriend people—no matter where they are from—and far more advantageous to have many good friends than to do the opposite. I find other forms of language fascinating, and moreover, I find other cultures, especially their foods, to be even more fascinating and enjoyable.

From very early childhood, I've learned by watching how other people behave toward each other. We all learn certain aspects of life through this interactive manner. I've also learned to keep an open mind, which includes the fact that even if I may not understand or agree with everything others do and—this is important—as long as what these people do is morally and socially acceptable, then it's okay. After all, that is what makes the world go round. We all make the team, know what I mean!

An uninformed person needs to read books. Read, read, read! That is exactly what I was told from the beginning of my abilities. Reading can help open up a person's eyes to a whole new level of thinking.

Once a person is able to thoroughly comprehend the subject matter he or she is reading, then that person is able to ascertain the validity of the author's writings. That way a person can make better decisions without relying on the help of other people who might have their own personal opinions or agendas. "Read lots of books," is what I believe to be were my parents exact words . . . Read, read, read informative periodicals and reputable newsmagazines. Learn for yourself too.

Life's Lessons Are the Test of Time

As I recall the times back when I was so young, I remember how important it was to both my parents that we kids learn the many meaningful lessons of life and to embrace them. Both of my parents certainly had the energy and conviction to teach us kids on a steady and continuous daily basis, and that was good too, because they certainly had designs on teaching us kids these lessons for a long time to come. So much so that they were literally teaching us every single day while reiterating the lessons we had learned from the days before. From the very beginning of birth, we are all being taught certain aspects of proper functioning in the world around us.

We all learn through both verbal communication and observation of others' examples. Everyone of us. In other words, young as well as older people have and will continue to mimic others. As when I was a child living in a world of wonderment, we kids did just exactly that. We joined the other neighborhood children and ultimately would proceed to mimic these new friends in our quest for fun. After all, mimicry is the best form of flattery.

Young kids can heed warnings very well, like, for instance, "Don't touch that!" Of course that one and many other well-known and often-used little ditties were a constant daily reminder for us inexperienced children to hear, ultimately until we developed and adopted these cautious mannerisms for ourselves. After a while we not only remembered the rules of the road for ourselves, but we also adopted that mimicry habit of reminding others to be careful.

As I look back on it now with a much more broader perspective, being four years old wasn't so bad at all. After all, everything that life has to offer a child is entirely brand new, and therefore a child is never bored for lack of originality. The way I see it, even if the child has seen the subject of interest before, pretty much everything is still on the brand-new and exciting-to-see list for quite some time to come yet.

Little kids are great. I'm sure that most everyone can testify to the nature of young children. Children everywhere around the world display many similarities in behavior, whereby they all share a common characteristic that is totally unto them: It's their storytelling abilities. First of all, most children will usually start off telling the story with great elation, highlighted with their own personal, highly demonstrative way of explaining the most incredible yet common occurrence that they have witnessed. More times than not, these young storytellers will end their narratives feeling great satisfaction that they were being quite helpful by explaining the best parts of the story. Precious!

I personally love to watch how the very young act while explaining how old they are. Typically, three-year-old kids and sometimes as old as six-year-olds won't just tell you how old they are; they'll assist you further in the understanding of their age by holding up the appropriate number of their little fingers, as high into the air as possible with perhaps just a slight bit of awkwardness, all the while explaining just how old three is. Sometimes this display is accompanied with a simple soft voice. "This many." We sure can't get anymore accurate than that.

FAMILY AND TRAVELING

My parents were simple working-class people, coming from simple folks. Both my parents were raised to adulthood without knowing the advantages that come from wealth—monetary wealth I mean to say. To be honest, they did not have even modest wealth.

My parents, though raised a few thousand miles apart geographically and with seven years apart in their ages, were both ultimately taught by their respective parents to do many similar gardening chores relating to eat-off-the-land or the literal garden-variety type of child rearing. Homesteading was the normal practice for both my parents and their respective siblings growing up.

My dad was born in 1919 in Oklahoma. He was basically just another healthy newborn in the eyes of his dutiful and cautiously concerned nurses. However, to his proud parents, my grandpa Otis and grandma Lu, he was a much-welcomed sight. They were elated to have yet another strong boy in their already growing family.

My dad's oldest brother, Virgil, was born thirteen years before my dad, in 1906. Following next in order was Marshall, who was born in 1908, and then Clarence, born in 1912. By the time my dad was five years old, he would have two younger sisters as well, the beautiful and adorable Helen and Lillian.

The years living in Oklahoma were short for my dad, and by the time he had barely familiarized himself with the sights and sounds and all of the smells that come from living in a particular area, his immediate family packed up and moved out west to the great state of California—Santa Cruz, to be more precise.

The story of my grandparents' travel out west has never been narrated to me in great detail. I can confirm that they traveled from Oklahoma to California in the early 1920s per the limited amount I was told, so therefore I can only hypothesize and speculate as to how they actually traveled out west.

One of the more common routes to travel back in the mid to late 1920's, if traveling by automobile, would have been the famous Route 66, which was one of the first main thoroughfares built for long-distance travel. However, this particular route, while destined to be widely popular, was nonexistent at the time my grandparents were traveling out west, which means they must have traveled some other smaller roads. There were very few interstate highways back in the early 1920's, especially ones paved with asphalt.

FYI: In 1904 there were less than 150 miles of paved roads in the U.S. It takes time and effort to build the infrastructure, i.e. city and interstate highways. Horace Greeley, being a well know newspaper editor of the New-York Tribune as well as being a politician of the 19th century. Horace Greeley who also happened to be friends with William Seward - who in his own right was greatly responsible for the purchase of the Alaskan territory back in the mid-19th century- is credited with popularizing the catch phrase "Go West. Young Man" during the early 1880's.

Even though my grandparents weren't exactly flush with money, they must have had some money saved up in order to make such a long and arduous trek—for that time—across several states. They weren't exactly rolling in the dough so-to-speak, after-all, they were just simple, hardworking people making a new start at life in a whole new different part of the country. Very brave indeed. It reminds me of some other wonderful people I know who traveled all the way from the most beautiful country of Greece in order to start their lives in a totally new area of the world. Unable to speak the english language at first, these strong willed and determined greek emigrants quickly adapted to there new surroundings and ultimately making the best of a new life. But I digress, as this too is another story of great interest for another time.

I certainly would like to have heard the full story regarding the particulars of how my Grandpa Otis, and Grandma Lu along with all six of their children in tow, traveled out to California in the early 1920's. Of course the silver-screen movies, as they were referred to then, often show how some people traveled in those days, whereby giving me something to work with. With those movie visuals I can hypothesize as to how my grandparents may have traveled back then, and which route they may have taken. Perhaps they took the plank roads of the sandy southwest or maybe an easier, safer northern route.

It's highly conceivable that my grandparents traveled in a semi modern vehicle of that time. If they did, it's likely that they traveled in what was known as a tin lizzie or some other sort of jalopy of the day. Certainly crossing the more precarious southern route would include having to negotiate the inabilities of other would-be travelers on roads. This southern route would have been a perfect route about twenty years in their future, but in those days the roads of the southwest were nothing more than a few planks of lumber stretched out over many miles. Imagine what it was like to have just gotten a car for the first time. Who really knew how to drive a car back then, let alone how to negotiate on coming traffic.

Yet again, perhaps my grandparents traveled by means of a Conestoga wagon, thereby taking a more traditional northwest route, capitalizing on the wide-open space at the time. Perhaps their desire to get out to the West Coast was greater yet, and they used the smaller prairie schooner to speed-travel the 1,200-plus miles. That would certainly have saved them some serious travel expense.

However, over the years I have since concluded that my grandparents must have traveled by means of some form of early-style touring car like those depicted in the movies of that time. This would certainly lend more accuracy to my tin-lizzie supposition.

Ultimately, my grandparents did travel westward, making their passage safely all the way to the great Pacific Ocean. Upon their immediate arrival, my grandparents settled in to their new location quite comfortably after finding a nice one-acre piece of land on the outskirts of the small community of Santa Cruz to settle into. My dad, along with his siblings were quick to adapt and were raised almost entirely on the small homestead while learning about life's lessons for themselves. Living on the outskirts of the undeniably beautiful city of Santa Cruz must have been a dream come true.

This little piece of land they called home was situated within the vicinity of the Santa Cruz headlands, nestled just below the beautiful Santa Cruz Mountains, and would became their home for many years to come. Moreover, this wonderful piece of farmland was located on a higher portion of the main headlands, providing everyone who was there with a beautiful 180 degree panoramic view of the great blue Pacific Ocean.

Back in my Grandpa Otis' youthful days, an American politician by the name of Horace Greeley, who was also at one time, editor of the New-York Tribune, is credited with popularizing the catch phrase of that era, "Go West young man, and grow with the country." My Grandpa Otis was a young man when he first heard those words when they were still being used as an incentive. Grandpa Otis may not have been a young man at the time he and Grandma Lu traveled out west with their young family, but then again, what does age have to do with it.

OLD SCHOOL

In the fall of 1930 my horticulturally gifted grandpa Otis passed away, leaving my grandma Lu to continue on with the duties of raising the four younger children that still remained under her care while staying on the little homestead. The four children included my dad, who was eleven years old at the time; his older brother Clarence; and his two younger sisters, Helen and Lillian—all four of whom had been raised to know the art of self-reliance in regards to the many aspects of agronomy.

However, during my father's mid-teenage years, the beekeeping, crop cultivation, and basically pretty much all of the other homesteading activities grew tiresome for him, and soon he realized that he needed to leave the farm. I don't know the exact time in his life that he realized this epiphany, however I do know that by his seventeenth birthday, in 1936, he had asked for and received his mother's written consent to enlist in the United States Navy. From that point on, my dad became the household breadwinner sending my grandmother three quarters of his monthly paycheck. Whenever my dad volunteered to talk about his naval experiences, he would always refer highly towards the military life and how it gave him many opportunities, which included taking financial care of his mother.

Just five years after my dad enlisted, while stationed at Pearl Harbor, Hawaii, at the age of twenty-two, he witnessed firsthand the horrors of the infamous Pearl Harbor attack on December 7, 1941. He never really talked much about his experiences he had while serving in the US Navy, especially not about any of the battles, even though I know for a fact he was aboard ship for many of the actual battle engagements in the Pacific Theater during the war. That's no big surprise really, as he never talked to us kids much about his siblings and family life while growing up in Santa Cruz either. If us kids wanted to know anything about his experiences during that time, we had to ask specific, and direct questions in order to get any real type of articulate response. And though my dad chose to be silent about his time in the US Navy, specifically the many different conflicts he took part in as an NCO, I was and am nonetheless proud of him and his seemingly mysterious past.

BEING PROUD FOR THE RIGHT REASONS

Perhaps another reason I was so proud of my father was that when ever we drove through a military guard post- passing by a guard gate in order to access the military grounds is to be getting permission to enter onto a military base- and in doing so, we were practically saluted every time we went through these military gates. That was extremely cool for my two brothers and me; it was always a very big deal to us whenever we passed through those military-guarded gates.

Of course now and again, whenever my dad did talk about the war, he referred to the opposing forces with respect and impressed upon us the importance of not holding grudges against people who were doing their duty as well. This lesson was only strengthened by his actions as he had form several very good friendships with people of the very same nationalities he had fought against in the war. Lesson learned.

My dad was a tall man. Even at a young age, I realized that he was taller than most. As I got older, I would understood better just how big he was. He was six feet two inches tall and weighed somewhere around 230 pounds. Now even though my dad was big and tall, I truly believe that I was more proud of and more impressed by my dad, not simply because of his vertical advantage, but rather because of his willingness to stand with many of his contemporaries and fight back against the tyranny and unjust actions of others in war.

After twenty years active service in the US Navy, my dad decided to retire out. Because he retired out instead of leaving another way, he still retained his rights to go onto any US military base to purchase food, clothing, gasoline, or practically anything else a person might need, which included major household appliances, all for a reduced price. This particular type of entitlement belonged to all personnel presently serving in the military and to people like my dad who had served for a certain conditional amount of time. So this should explain why we were always passing through military guard posts. I hope so anyway.

I loved going to these different military posts. It was like a whole other world every time.

Now that my dad was no longer in the military, he obviously didn't wear any type of uniform anymore suddenly becoming a civilian, and certainly nothing to indicate he had ever served in the military, or that he was a survivor of such an infamous event in history for that matter. Still though, nearly every time we entered a military base, no matter where it was, the military guards standing and maintaining the guard gate, allowing only the authorized in and out, would not only motion us on through the entrance gate but would also come to a full and complete attention for just a split second. In doing so, they'd give us (really to my dad) a sharp, military salute. Very impressive indeed. Very impressive at any age. And it didn't happen just once in a while but practically every time we went through those gates. That, is a certain kind of respect that I embraced early on as well. I mean, it was perfectly clear to anyone who saw these guardsmen saluting that they held my dad in the highest regards. It was a type of fraternity for both men and women who know the realities of this rather esoteric world.

Because of my inquisitive nature, I once asked my dad why these guards were always saluting us when we drove through the gate. He simply explained to us kids that it was in their training to do so. It was all that simple. But I like to think that these young military personnel did their own math and deduced that my dad and all the other inactive military personnel deserved a certain amount of respect and admiration.

I always got such a thrill out of watching those guards salute us like that nearly every time—or, I should say, saluting my dad to be more accurate and respectful.

PROUD OF MY CANADIAN CONNECTIONS

My mother's immediate family was from the northern portion of the Americas, where my grandma G was born in 1903 and raised a citizen of Canada, while my grandpa G was born in 1902 and raised in beautiful Illinois. Grandpa G or Henry meet my grandma G or Arilla, in the early twenties and married each other in 1926, and choosing to reside on my grandma G's family land, where my mother was born that December in a little wood house with no running water or electricity.

Having no running water in the house made things plenty complicated, which also meant no indoor bathroom. No problem, though—apparently they didn't have to walk too far to get to the outhouse, so that's obviously a good thing for them. Right? Maybe thirty-five yards or so to the outhouse. Oh, and by the way, the doctor in that vicinity made house call and would be a the residence all night or all day if necessary. Sort of crazy sounding; the doctor of that area coming to their house to help with the birthing, and not the other way around as is practiced today. This is no-doubt during that era, back when resident doctors made house calls, and not the other way around. We can see how that worked out. All's well, because my mother and grandmother survived this ordeal just fine. My mother grew up to be a very strong and athletic young girl, and truly a very wonderful person too I might add.

My mother's younger brother, Philip, was born in the spring of 1928, just a little more than a full year after my mother's birth. And in the 1930s my mother's two sisters arrived—Carolyn in 1930 and Betty Ellen in 1931. My mother and her siblings were raised to know how to handle themselves on a farm and how to care for livestock in a farming atmosphere—a lesson in how to live off the land, so to speak. Only it wasn't really a lesson as much as it was a way of life.

SOCIALIZING IS A GOOD THING

Communication is the absolute beginning to a better understanding. It's best to know something about what we attempt to teach. And both my parents knew farming; that's for sure.

My first home was located in the Santa Clara Valley farming community of Campbell, California. It's certainly no farming community today, but back in 1956 it was pretty much all farmland.

In the late 1950s and early 1960s, Campbell, being one of several small cities in that vicinity, was just at its infancy, about to begin improving and growing in size right along with all the other fast-paced developing infrastructure going on at the time throughout the Santa Clara Valley. As with everything, with growth comes changes, and the Santa Clara Valley was about to experience a very rapid growth.

During those days there were only a handful of cities in the valley region—very old cities with really cool names like Santa Clara, San Jose, Los Gatos, Los Altos, Alviso, Alum Rock, Willow Glen, Sunnyvale, Mountain View, Monte Sereno, Morgan Hill, Saratoga, Cupertino, Milpitas, Campbell, and Gilroy, of the Gilroy Garlic Festival acclaim. I hope I got 'em all. Of course many new communities have sprung up in the past fifty-five-plus years.

I certainly was living in and around a fascinating and fast-growing community. It was growing so fast that within three months of my birth, my family was packing up and moving to a new city, Sunnyvale, which was not that far in miles from where we were living before, just more conveniently closer in relative nature to other special interest of my parents. Now of course at this time I had no real concerns regarding this particular move; however, it turned out that our new home was a lot closer in travel distance to my dad's new job as well. So that was why my parents chose to move.

Obviously I was too young at the time to realize any of my new home's qualifying attributes. However, as I got older, I realized exactly what my two older brothers were enjoying. While this new home wasn't any larger than our older home—in fact the yard was smaller—it did have railroad tracks with trains running nearby. In fact it was a series of railroad tracks that ran both commuter trains as well as large, heavy freight trains, and the tracks were just on the other side of our backyard fence. That was pretty cool. Plus the Moffett Federal Airfield—or Moffett Field Navy Base, as we called it—was just 3 to 4 miles away, putting our shopping center that much closer in travel time. But the best part of it was that Moffett Field had planes taking off and landing all the time. I mean this really couldn't get any better for us kids. Of course this would explain why there were so many airplanes and jets flying around overhead. Yeah, it really was a pretty cool place to grow up around.

San Francisco, California, is undoubtedly one of the most famous cities in the world, and it was just up the road from our new house, around thirty-nine miles to the north along the very same peninsula as that of Sunnyvale. San Francisco; the famous city being right up the highway from our home was nothing short of great. Once again, at this time I had no real idea just how far away San Francisco was in time or distance; as far as I knew, San Francisco was right up the highway from our house, and that was great—great because we were frequent visitors at the San Francisco Zoo.

I don't exactly remember very much about those particular outings, due to my age at the time, however the pictures and the corresponding stories in my family's possession are enough for me to share a good story from time to time.

Socializing with people we met during our outings presented no real problems for me, especially once I got a better handle on verbal skills.

Once my communication skills had improved, my socializing became much easier. And once I mastered the language of communication, there was no keeping me back from talking to anyone and everybody. I suppose some of the adults and perhaps some of the older kids as well, may have at one time or another considered me to be some what of a loquacious child. Of course it's natural that I would have a little trouble at the beginning with the challenging dynamics of learning how to verbally communicate with others, especially coming from the preverbal state that I had been accustomed to. It would be due to the patience of everyone around me that I ultimately and rather quickly learned how to communicate properly. And of course by that time, I was off to the races, learning more and more, and talking everyone's ears off.

Everything at this young age was still quite new to me, and I was extremely fascinated and interested in discovering just what all these different things around me were and just what all this stuff I was looking at was. My simple curiosity took me in the direction of using the power of endless questions, specifically the ever-so-popular go-to "What's that?" question. Yes indeed, the power of endless questions … and they worked too. "What's that?"

PAY ATTENTION NOW OR PAY LATER

My mom and dad were fairly outgoing people by most standards, my dad more so than my mom. My dad just loved to talk to most anybody, even strangers at just about any gas station. On the other hand, my mother was the total opposite and was more of a listener. She would engage others in an articulate conversation at any time, but she preferred to listen. She was definitely a very good listener.

Both my parents were outdoorsy, so it was a normal routine for us to head out on any given Saturday or Sunday for a drive. Every time we went out like this, we ended up meeting lots of different people, many of them doing the same thing we were doing, which was casually driving around the countryside looking for a spot to have a picnic. These weekend excursions were a mix of fun and family bonding while at the same time providing one of those life lessons I needed to learn so I too could eventually pass the test of time with ease. Both my parents wanted us kids to know the outside world, so to speak, and they thought one of the most important lessons in life was to master the ability to get along with others. One of the ways to accomplish this is to see other people as they are. Their plan was for us to visit places in our free time and get to see what other people do for a living or at their own leisure. Granted, we always went on the weekends, and most people who worked the traditional workweek of Monday through Friday were not working; however, not everyone had the luxury of working nine-to-five jobs.

While out on our excursions we might stop at a public park and watch a ball game or eat our picnic at one of the nearby state parks. We often made stops at our local dairy. Even though we got most of our dairy products from the neighborhood grocery store on the military naval base, we would still get some fresh milk right from the dairy farmer. My favorite times were when we would just arbitrarily pick a random, open-to-the-public horse stable to visit, though we wouldn't necessarily have lunch there. Wherever we traveled, there was always a nice place to sit down and enjoy our picnic, maybe under some tall oaks.

Inevitably, we would meet other people doing the same, and we'd start talking. I realized that making friends is easy to do. I learned that some people we met were just as happy and eager to befriend us as we were eager to be their friends. Sometimes we would run into these same people at another location under different circumstances—a complete surprise. It was great to see people whom we barely knew but, because we had befriended each other, were now our friends everywhere we went.

Happy Landings

I mean seriously, what kid isn't excited about seeing airplanes taking off and landing all the time? That, going to a really fun zoo, and visiting equestrians on the weekend were just a few of the fun things we did. Oh yeah, I have to say my hometown and the surrounding communities in the area turned out to be a pretty cool place to grow up! We made sure of it.

The whole of the Santa Clara Valley floor was engaged chiefly in agriculture for the first fifty years of the twentieth century. However, after the Second World War the baby boomers sprang into action. The slow and steady expansion turned into a full-on urban sprawl by the early 1960s. New homes, schools, hospitals, museums, small businesses, large businesses, and all sorts of businesses in between sprung up all over the valley practically every day. Though eclectic at first glance, this mix of both agriculture and industrial commerce would not coexist for long. A really big change in the surrounding landscape was about to occur— so big that it would literally push the once thriving and renowned agriculture industry out of existence in the Santa Clara Valley.

However, for the late 1950s and early 1960s, the valley would, for the most part, remain a well-balanced, light-industrial, blue-collar community with a plethora of fruit-tree orchards throughout the region. It was quite common to have twenty acre fruit orchards right down the road. Many different varieties of fruit tree orchards were still growing throughout the Santa Clara valley. Prunes, apricots, and cherries were the dominant varieties in our area. I thankGod for that too because for as much as I like apricots and plums, my personal favorite happens to be cherries. I love those different cherry varieties, and we always got to eat them during the various times of the season.

All these different fruit tree orchards were scattered throughout the valley region, completely invisible to most people living in the nearby communities. I don't understand how they could drive by and not take notice. Some people, like my family, took advantage of this opportunity and purchased the ripe, fresh-picked fruit right from the farmers. The people who bought from the fruit stands may not have been the socializing type, but fruit-stand conversations are generally short in nature anyway. My parents took full advantage of this opportunity every time the fruit or vegetables were in season.

The local children in the area, including my two brothers and me, knew all too well about these fruit orchards, as we considered them foremost as playgrounds. We'd often ride our bicycles into the orchard only to be chased off by the farmer. Inevitably, one by one, these large fruit orchards began to disappear in order to make room for housing developments and expansion. The infrastructure i.e. construction of homes, schools, museums, retail stores, and other businesses were all necessary to accommodate and meet the needs of the rapidly growing community.

MOFFETT AIRFIELD

My dad completed twenty years of active service in the U.S. Navy, and during this time he managed to achieve the rank of chief petty officer. And as I said before, because he retired out of the navy, we were entitled to shop for food, clothing, and pretty much any other household necessities at the Moffett Field Navy Base, which netted huge monetary savings for my parents. Of course we weren't the only ones allowed to do this. This privilege belonged to anyone active in the military and their immediate family members as well as to anyone who retired out of the military with certain privileges for the family members. The advantage to shopping on military bases is quite obvious; patrons will always pay far less for an item than they would off base, or in the civilian world, as it was called.

I don't exactly remember how old I was when I got my first military ID, but at one point or another an ID is necessary for everyone in the family. There are fewer regulations in the civilian world of shopping than on a military base; that's for sure. Still, when we shopped on base, it was less crowded, and that translated into shorter lines, which translated even further into less boredom for us kids. It really was a win-win situation for my parents all around. Me too.

Practically every time my parents told us kids that we were going to go shopping over at the navy base, our reaction was "No problem. Let's go." We kids always enjoyed the trip out to Moffett Field if for nothing else than to watch as military jets and different kinds of airplanes took off and landed.

However, my brothers and I had another connection with this military post. For a while, we spent part of our days at the on-base day-care facility while both my parents worked. The day-care center was not too far from one of the front entrance gates and was within eyesight of the landing strip. This was where I got to witness a lot of the military activities first hand, like those military guards regulating the entrance gates, saluting just about every car as they gave permission to enter and sometimes stopping or detaining people for a short time.

Sometimes those guardsmen would really snap to attention and present an honest-to-goodness military salute to us, the type of salute seen in movies, like when saluting a commodore, the type of salute that displays a lot of respect. Most times, though, their salutes were a simple gesture of authority and approval with a casual yet enthusiastic finger pointing in the direction the car is to proceed, as if saying "Go on ahead; go on through." Oh yeah, they all wore sidearms too, and that certainly added a big coolness factor.

Another really great attraction to this place and certainly one of the most interesting aspects about this military compound was that it housed three huge airship hangars. These airship hangars were huge. The oldest of the three hangars was first built long before I was born, back in the earlier half of the twentieth century when Americans and other parts of the world were still considering air travel by means of the slow yet reliable dirigibles. To be more exact, the building was constructed and open for business by 1933. So when I saw the building many years later, it was old with an extremely powerful allure and distinctive appearance. It gave me the kind of thrill level that was right up there with seeing the Golden Gate Bridge, which by the way was something I had personally seen with my family on many occasions. Only difference is that I got to see all of the cool looking activities on the navy base nearly everytime I was at the daycare center.

The two other airship hangars were built ten years after the first hanger, which would have been during the time of the Second World War. All three of these airship hangars were equally huge in stature, each standing just as tall and majestic as the next one. However, those two later built hangars, Hangar 2 and Hangar 3, were merely functional, and not nearly as intriguing as the older Hangar 1. The fact that to this day all three of these seemingly old and outdated hangar's are still in complete functioning order is a true testimony to the master craftsmanship of the construction crew that originally built these majestic structures and to the crew of people over the years towards the proper preservation with tender loving care to keep these now antiquated building up and functioning through the ages.

On a few occasions from time to time, when not housing actual airships, the hangars - being large buildings and therefore a great place for special ceremonies and events- were used in that regard. On more than a few occasions the command-base authorities allowed certain festivities to take place inside Hangar 1. These building actually occupied a lot of land space, making them ideal for large crowds to gather while offering a safe venue free from the threat of harsh weather spoiling the activities. Funny thing, though, these hangars were so big and tall, that actual weather conditions would form, occurring naturally inside. Clouds!

I personally never witnessed the phenomenon myself, but I had heard on more than one occasion that clouds would form inside these hangars and sometimes deliver unwanted precipitation down on the workers' heads below. I guess that's one of the few times it's necessary to use an umbrella inside.

WHAT'S WITH THESE CHIPS?

The Santa Clara Valley was growing in population as well, all due to the industrial acceleration and the many different businesses moving quickly into the area, causing an exponential growth rate, resulting in an extremely fast pace construction boom.

It seems that no matter how time moves on for each person, eventually there is going to be some type of change. Now then, with that said, in the late 1960s and early 1970s, the majority of this valley would morph seemingly overnight, claiming the famous Silicon Valley moniker. It had been some years in the making albeit, but nonetheless, the electronic industry was quickly beginning to plant a firm foothold in this valley floor.

Not only electronics businesses but many other businesses of all varying types were popping up everywhere. This type of snowball effect always encourages many other businesses to form in order to accommodate the influx of the many people and their personal needs as well.

All this of course translates into the need for new homes and new schools, but I already mentioned that, didn't I? Hold on a minute, though. That's part of learning. Hearing something over a few times really can make it sink into your memory better.

Though actually I'm jumping ahead of events as they chronologically occurred. I still have to recount for the happenings of the early 1960s first. Always start at the beginning, as it is a good practice to follow when telling as story.

MOVING TO A BRAND-NEW STATE

On this one particular spring day in 1960, just like a scene out of movie, my dad came home from work and told us kids that the decision had been made for us, as a family, to move to Alaska in a few months, Kodiak, Alaska, to be more exact. I'm guessing right now, but at the time I must have thought, *Wherever that is ...* if even that. After all, I had just celebrated my fourth birthday only a few weeks before receiving this exciting news.

We had no atlas or world map to help my brothers and me obtain any real visual idea as to where Kodiak, Alaska, truly was, adding an even deeper mystery to this sudden and exciting news. I had no idea where or, for that matter, *what* this all meant. Making matters worse, I couldn't even pronounce these new words.

Truth be told, I was okay with all this excitement because I trusted my family, and if they were excited about this and okay with it, then I would be too. That was the way it was.

Not long after the big news of us moving to another state, some of our relatives began to visit us at our house much more often, as they discussed our move with great interest. I was old enough at this time to understand many words but only some of the concepts that the older folks were talking about. Everything they had to say about this new place and its mysterious surrounding area was always exciting and interesting to hear about, to say the least, especially the stories that two of my uncles liked to tell. They told us kids stories of what to expect in this new frontier called Alaska, the forty-ninth state of the Union, a brand-new state.

During this particular time, very little general public knowledge was known about Alaska. No one in my immediate family, including my two adventurous uncles, had ever been to Alaska before that I knew of. These well-meaning relatives were simply telling us kids stories about what they had heard and read. Almost every story and every concept they told us regarding Alaska and it's frontier had us captivated.

Systematically over the course of three full months, my relatives, living in or around the immediate area, had begun more regular and constant visits to our house in preparation for our upcoming quest, as us kids would sit still long enough to hear maybe one more wild, adventurous story from either one or both of our uncles. It could have been a story told to us previously by the other uncle, but with the new description and a grander spin on it. Whether it was Uncle Al or Uncle Marshall, it really didn't matter; they were both highly opinionated regarding the many varieties of fish and wild animals that lived in the far north. They seemed to be trying to out duel each other in their stories by adding yet more nonexistent species to the Kodiak area by means of utter hyperbole. Still though, a story told by either uncle was extremely intriguing to listen to. Besides, I was too young to actually realize for myself the validity, or understand the validity regarding much of the nuances in their stories. I sure loved those stories they told us kids, every single on.

Both my two uncles and pretty much everyone else told us kids of the varying small creeks to mighty rivers that flowed throughout the region and of all the different fish that swam these waters. Some of these fish were supposedly large enough to break fishing poles right out of a man's hands. Therefore it stood to reason that since both my uncles, being avid amateur fishermen themselves, were excited for us, and telling us stories was their way of getting involved and helping us kids prepare for what they perceived as a thrill of a lifetime. After all, Alaska was a long, long ways away. Well, they didn't exactly use those words, but that was pretty much what I had imagined when they said, "Way up north!"

Having heard the many different stories my two uncles told us, stories of all those strange creatures living in the waters and walking the land, were pretty much all I had to go on. They told us kids stories about creatures that many people, including my two adventurous uncles, had never seen with their own two eyes before. There was no such thing as the Internet back then, and not everyone subscribed to *National Geographic*.

Just a quick heads-up here: this was during a time when actually very few items were even made from plastic. The pocket-size transistor radio was soon to become hugely popular. The transistor itself had been discovered in 1947, only thirteen years earlier. Also in those days, most men wore a dress shirt and tie every day, sometimes even while mowing the front lawn or doing some other type of arduous yard work around their home.

During those day, all of us kids and including the adults as well, would marvel at the occasional sonic boom echoing from the sky above. Back then it was fairly common to hear sonic booms echoing throughout the immediate sky. The loud booms were an aftereffect created by jets flying faster than the speed of sound and thus breaking the sound barrier, creating booming sounds that could literally rattle the dinner plates in the cupboards at home. Breaking the sound barrier over populated areas is outlawed these days, but it sure did make for a lasting memory for me—obviously, since I'm still talking about it.

Now I was as enthusiastic about this epic move to the new state as anyone else, if for nothing else than being caught up in the emotional enthusiasm that everyone around me had been expressing so much of during those exciting weeks prior to us moving. It seemed to me that during these few months preceded our impending departure, everyone around us shared in our excitement about our up-coming quest, so obviously that made me excited in turn, even though at this time, I still had no real understanding or vision of what things would be like in the near future, or what to expect two months later. Hello ... I was only four years old.

Just how much understanding of a certain concept does a four-year-old fully comprehend anyway? First of all, it takes a little extra time for children to absorb and then comprehend when they first come in contact. Case in point, I knew absolutely nothing about why we were moving. Why my dad's company was sending him and his entire family to a place called Kodiak, I did not know! The name and proper pronunciation—Ko-dee-ak—of our new town-to-be was about the only part I truly understood. And even that part of it took me a little extra time to memorize and get untangled—not the pronunciation so much as remembering it was in Alaska. The new place we're moving to is called Kodiak. Wait a minute, though; it's Alaska after all, right? And the town is called Kodiak, and it's an island. And the entire island is also called Kodiak. Great, that's good to know. Alaska … got it. Kodiak Island … got it. Let's go!

Of course once I understood the differences between the two, I started working on pronouncing both these two new words a little better. Even though I thought I was pretty good at pronouncing the names of those new places with fairly clear diction for my age, I was still having a little difficulty, thus prompting me to work those new words practically on a daily bases, which included evenings. I may have actually just liked the sound of saying those new words a lot too. Once I achieved proficiency in pronouncing these new words, or at least as close as I was ever going to get at that age, those new words just seemed to flowed out of my mouth. Kodiak … Kodiak, Alaska. Yes, I do believe it is possible—in fact I'm quite sure—that I practiced pronouncing those new words right up to the point of testing my parents' patience to the limits. That would have to go for my two brothers as well; they had to endure my persistence too. Once I was fluent in those two new words, I began to work on my understanding of what exactly was meant by saying "new state."

During those several weeks leading up to our actually travel date, I was busy practicing my diction by reciting over and over Kodiak, Alaska. For awhile there it was Alaska this and Alaska that, Kodiak this and Kodiak that. That must have sounded annoying to some, but it was great for me because the repetition made it easier for me to pick up on how to properly enunciate the new words. I eventually realized that pretty much everyone around was willing to lend gentle constructive criticism to me at the appropriate time, when it mattered most. Of course that makes it a lot easier. It was around this time that I first became aware that some of my newfound words that I thought were just fluidly flowing out of my mouth were in truth sounding more like twaddle.

Everyone is slightly different, and speech forms differently for each of us. I too eventually became aware of my own speech patterns and barely-there diction, and as most of us do, I began a conscious effort to improve upon myself, using my relatives' constructive criticism. Albeit I had some catching up to do all right.

I think one of the more interesting things to come out of all of this was that I was beginning to learn another language as well. *Kodiak* means "island" in the native tongue of the area's indigenous people.

THE GREAT ICEBOX

Before we left for Alaska, my aunts and uncles made sure all three of us boys had a pretty clear picture—for what can be deciphered by little kids—of this exciting new frontier. "You are all going to have so much fun up there in Alaska, the time of your life," they would say. That type of gentle encouragement came from my aunties. They were always encouraging and supportive to me. How profound those words were, because that's exactly how it was.

I loved those aunts and uncles of mine. They were so great. My aunts were all pretty much the same, always loving and being really sweet, so concerned about our future living conditions. My uncles were loving too but way tougher. My uncles' stories were more along the lines of survival … I guess. Two of my more boisterous uncles—Al and Marshal—were like night and day but were both as right as rain with the outdoors. Their stories were so great to listen to but also very scary. While one uncle was entirely serious about the matter at hand, the other one was about equally as funny as he was smart and charming.

Both uncles, the two who did all the storytelling, were experienced amateur sports fishermen, and whereby both had read many stories about the Alaskan frontier. These two would go on and on in dissertations based on their personal knowledge regarding what types of fish were running in those rivers and streams "up there." It was when those two uncles started swapping stories and describing in much greater detail their firsthand experiences that the stories got really good.

Though I may have tried to pay close attention, truth be told, most of those stories went right over my head. I would be confused and excited at the same time. They would have me interested in every single story up until they started talking about certain variables of casting or some other boring talk of hooks or how the best knots are tied. Boring!!! But then as soon as they started up with their stories of actually fishing and catching fish the size of this, or the size of that and other stories of further adventures, is when their stories all started to sound exciting again, and making more sense too. But then really, wasn't that their objective, to mix the boring into the exciting to get me to learn something? I mean, it eventually worked, because I know the names of those hooks and I still know how to tie those many different types of knots I had ultimately been taught.

It's pretty simple to imagine just what thoughts must have been swirling around in my head—really simple as a matter of fact. I mean, I was at that point in my life where I could have been in awe of practically everything I saw, touched, and heard.

Each and every child experiences a certain amount of time lapse between birth and a cognizant state of being. My personal awakening was somewhere around four years of age. I already said that, didn't I? But what I didn't say was that, just like most other people, I will from time to time get a feeling or flash of a memory, triggered perhaps by looking at an inanimate object. This feeling is perhaps a blurred memory of sorts, one of the slight outer memories of my pre cognizant period trying to come to the surface, where I might make some sort of sense of it.

I thought I'd share that; after all, it's just a thought. Think about it.

MY UNCLES' STORIES

Thinking back on it, I am more aware now than ever that my aunts and uncles, especially my uncles, were probably more excited about us moving to Alaska than we were. Still, I was raring and ready to go to Alaska at the drop of a hat, especially after hearing one or both of my uncles' stories about all the strange and different animals we would soon be witnessing, like large congregations of walruses. We had very few pictures to look at, and without pictures we were once again put in a position of relying on the powers of our imaginations and accurate storytellers. The Internet was not available back then, and nobody thought to bring pictures.

Now it would have been quite possible that we saw walruses at the San Francisco Zoo or perhaps at the Oakland Zoo across the bay. After all, we went to both zoos. But I do not recall if either zoo had walruses. Anyway, with the way my storytelling uncles described these creatures, I ended up imagining something way different from what walruses actually are. I mean come on, animals that lived in the deep, cold waters and sunbathed on ice floes?

My uncles' descriptions of the various Alaskan creatures were absolutely captivating yet incredibly scary at the same time. My uncles even told us kids stories about a sea creature that lived exclusively in the cold Arctic waters, like walruses, but instead of having two large front teeth, this creature, a narwhal, had just one long tooth. This particular Arctic whale only grows to about fourteen feet long, which is rather small for a whale. Male narwhals will grow a single unicorn-type, spiraling tusk out their upper jaws like a tooth—a nine-foot-long tooth. Unicorns? My uncles were great story tellers with perhaps a subtle touch of hyperbole. I absolutely loved their stories and tales about Unicorn Whales.

It turned out that all the while I was hearing my uncles' fantastic and outlandish stories of walruses and whales, I was also receiving geography lessons. During my daily lessons, I was also being taught what it meant when people said "brand-new state." This concept was more than difficult for me to understand at the time; it also held no real interest for me. The idea that Alaska recently had become the forty-ninth state to be admitted into the United States of America had no real exciting appeal to me.

Think about it for a moment, though … This extremely large hunk of land, which is slightly more than twice the size of Texas, had been, since the actual purchase of the territorial Alaska back in 1867, which remained a territory of the United States until it became a state just months before our move north to Alaska. History in the making.

KNOW THE PARK RULES

Over time, most people will learn to recognize many different views regarding the various aspects of life. This eventual outcome has a great deal to do with their surrounding environment and conditions.

My family was about to move to a whole new area of the world, to a place that lived much differently from what we were used to. The lifestyle on Kodiak Island certainly was very different from the lifestyles of many other towns and cities around the world, yet it was also similar in many ways. When we arrived on the island, the first thing to do was to adapt to the locals' ways of living, so as not to upset the community or rock the boat, so to speak. It was up to us to fit in so as to make the most peaceful transition as possible. This would let these new neighbors know right from the beginning that we were interested in being a good addition to the community. I was taught early on that fellowship with others is good.

Now just like when visiting a park, every place has different laws, rules, and policies. Some parks allow pets or pets on leashes only, while some parks do not allow pets at all. Some parks allow campfires, while other parks prohibit such activities with extreme enforcement. So it was important for us to know and follow the general rules of the new location that we would be relocating to and calling home.

Two constant verbal reminders around our house were "It's better to be safe than sorry" and "Always be prepared." And with that in mind, I'll merely say that my parents were protective and knew that they would have to step up their game in that regard because of potential danger in the area we were moving to. Those stories my uncles told us kids were all pretty much truthful after all and were eventually confirmed by my parents ... to a degree. My parents told us that there were some pretty fabulous and unique plants as well as lots of wild animals up north in Kodiak, Alaska, and they taught us how to keep a good lookout for them, especially for the potentially dangerous wild animals.

In doing so, they reassured us kids that Kodiak was a safe place to live and that my uncles' wild stories were meant to prepare us for this new land and the possible dangers that were everywhere. All those different crazy stories definitely did the trick. Very informative stories! The only flaw to their stories was that they were slightly exaggerated. My uncles added a little hyperbole to each story in order add that extra fear factor to an otherwise exciting story. The stories were their own renditions.

My parents played down all of these exaggerated stories and mostly taught us kids what to expect of the area, like the native words that were used, and told us stories about the famous lights of the aurora borealis and about people kayaking and swimming in the blue Alaskan waters. They taught us how to pronounce Native Alaskan Inuit words, like *kayak*, and taught us what the words meant, like how a *kayak* was a canoe-type boat used by the Native Alaskan people. *Umiak* is another Inuit word for boat and translates as "woman's boat." *Mukluks*, my favorite Inuit word to run around saying to everyone, means "boots." Mukluks ... what a fun word for any age. FYI, the Inuit language is one of the three base languages shared by the many different proud indigenous tribal people inhabiting this region for at least the past seven thousand years and counting.

BE WELL INFORMED

My parents made a great effort to get us kids familiar for this area and to help us kids prepare for what we were to expect. Both my parents seemed to know quite a bit about the area before we moved to the island. I already believed in my parents and thought that they were the smartest and seemed to know just about everything, so when they told me we were going to be all right, I believed them.

I mean, they knew when I was hungry and almost always knew exactly what I should eat. I say *almost* always because sometimes they fed me certain vegetables that I believe they knew I detested. They were near perfect otherwise. At one time or another they told me that glass was made from sand and that steel came from rocks. They even convinced me that paper was make from wood. Wood, does that make sense? Making paper from trees of all things!

It was eventually brought to my attention that my parents had lived on Kodiak Island once before, only a few years earlier, before I was born. Shortly after my parents were married, while my dad was still actively serving in the navy, they got a chance to be stationed on Kodiak Island, which ended up being one of my dad's last duty stations while serving in the navy. Though my parents quickly grew to love this island, my brother Tim was soon to be making his debut into the world. Alaska was still a territory at this time, and my dad's grand idea was that his soon to be arriving newborn son should be born in one of the recognized lower forty-eight states.

My brother Tim's impending birth was in part, good timing actually. My dad's two-year term of duty on the Kodiak Island naval post was wrapping up, so my parents decided to pack things up and move with my brother Fitzo, two years old at the time, back to the San Francisco Bay Area, where my dad was reassigned at Naval Air Station Alameda. This active naval station literally operated out of the San Francisco Bay, which was very close to where I too would be born in just another year and a half. My brother Tim was born in the second month of 1955, whereby at that time my dad had no idea that in less than four years Alaska would become the forty-ninth state of the United States of America.

My dad may have been overly cautious about his newborn son's political future or something to that effect. Since I never inquired further, I can only deduce that my dad must have been thinking at the time that if Tim was born in a US territory rather than in a state, Tim may have endured repercussions from it later in his life. I guess my dad had his reasons. I know we kids thought it would be cool to have been born in a territory ... especially Alaska!

The Abominable Snowman

As a young child, like any other child, getting used to my family's style of humor took a little … well, getting used to. My family's style of humor included adding innocent hyperbole to stories, such as those told to us kids about Alaska, to make the stories more memorable or at least more exciting. I was excited about moving to Alaska mainly because everyone else was excited about it too. But I also had the idea that I was maybe going to see these creatures in a cage, like at the zoo. We would soon see. Just the idea of moving to a new land was about all I needed to be excited.

Nothing would excite me more than to see the unicorn whales I was hearing so much about. But I have to admit, the story of the white snow ape screaming all night long on some lonely hillside was not my style. Nobody took the time to explain to me why this abominable snowman was screaming all the time in the first place. Yeah, I wasn't too interested in seeing the screaming snow ape at that time that's for sure. I just knew I didn't need any of that. Another good reason was that I personally had a harder time pronouncing *abominable* than any previously learned word.

Trusting my family members wholeheartedly was truly indispensable, even when some stories' validity was at stake.

All in all, scary stories or not, this new place we were moving to was sounding better and better to us kids every time we heard something spoken about it, especially as time inched closer to our departure date.

My two older brothers and I didn't possess any more childish bravado than any other average child of the same age; it was just the idea of moving to the newly admitted state of Alaska, where the night skies would light up from the activities of the aurora borealis.

The aurora borealis, or northern lights, are cosmic rays with electrically charged particles that flash light across the northern skies night and day. The promises of these beautiful ribbons of light dancing across the night sky and of many fishing adventures just waiting to be discovered were more than enough for us kids to want nothing more than to go immediately and without any further hesitation. Our anxious feeling at the time was like "All right already ... enough of the delays. Let's go!" We were convinced we'd heard enough by this time to have only one opinion about this new frontier called Alaska, and that opinion was that is going to be the best.

Without a doubt, each of us kids was absolutely ready for all of this, maybe even too ready if that's possible. It didn't take long at all for us to get that way with story after story of huge Kodiak brown bears roaming the lands, bald eagles flying high in the sky on the lookout for something to swoop down on, and those Arctic walruses. By the way, I found out later that there were no walruses anywhere near Kodiak Island. And as for the narwhals, well, like walruses, they were found in the deep Arctic Ocean and not anywhere near Kodiak Island.

It looks like some of those stories were meant to scare us kids into being aware of these creatures and many other types of dangers. And the closest I ever got to seeing anything remotely resembling an abominable snowman was the four snow guys and one snow girl we built in our own front yard. Each snow person represented one of our family members of course. We even made a snow dog to represent our protective police dog and best friend Lizzie.

Ultimately my understanding of this mythical screaming snow creature included the fact that it goes by many names, including Yeti. Let's put this into perspective. All that time I was having to get used to pronouncing *abominable,* which was crazy difficult for me to pronounce, like having a mouthful of peanuts with no clue. And all the while there were other simpler-to-pronounce words to use that meant the very same thing. That word Yeti, now that's a whole lot easier to pronounce. Maybe that's why no one told of this word.

But wait a minute now. Once again I'm sort of getting ahead of the story. I still need to narrate the journey to the distant Kodiak Island, Alaska.

Of course these events I just related actually did transpire, but for a while there, confusion and an overactive imagination on my part were my constant mind-set. Therefore I was mostly relying on my family to help me along and sort out any uncertainty. The imagination is both powerful and confusing for some.

OUR QUEST TO THE EXTREME NORTHWEST

With our impending departure date fast approaching, my brothers and I were asked to prepare ourselves by gathering together those things we most wanted to take with us. It was such a nice thought, yet just what would I, at four years old, want to take?

The decision of what to take was purely simple for my brother Tim and me, as our thoughts were those of children, simple and pure. Lizzie, our German shepherd dog and best friend, was the first and only choice. No argument. What else could I have that I would want to take? Well, maybe my stuffed toy elephant. That's right; I had a toy elephant for a hanger-on companion as well, but my very best friend was Lizzie. After all, just what does a child of four really need, other than his or her family, right? And Lizzie was family.

The thought of having Lizzie coming along with us on this adventure was paramount and actually made the idea of this trip more manageable and comfortable for all of us. Without a doubt, having a big dog like Lizzie riding along with us gave us all a great sense of security. FYI, at this time in the mid-twentieth century, German shepherds were often called police dogs. This was due in part to the negative effects and results of the Second World War and its repercussions on the rest of the world. Therefore, the general public was more comfortable with and preferred *police dog* to *German shepherd*, at least for a while.

Of course German shepherds were once favored to be police dogs, and why not? They're great. However, nowadays police dogs come in a number of different breeds, all physically fit and certified to work as a respected member of the police force, given the entitlement of an officer and well-deserved respect.

I was never confused about who Lizzie was. I gave it no never mind. She was my friend and a great dog and I trusted her. And besides being best friend to my family and the neighbor kids, she was also referred to as a police dog, and honestly that sounded really cool.

FLYING HIGH IN THE CLOUDY SKY

The day before my mother, my brothers, and I were to leave on our travels to Alaska (my dad had already left a couple of days before), we spent the night at my aunt Betty Ellen's house, which was much closer to the airport. Makes sense. It's at this time that I remember meeting some of my cousins for the first time. Or at least, this is when I first recall meeting my cousins. It all happened so fast. One day I was visiting my aunt and cousins, and the very next day we were flying high in the sky, heading for new prospects.

What word comes to mind that would best describe a four-year-old's feelings flying for the first time? *Awesome!*

I had butterflies in my stomach the first time I ever flew. Well, maybe they weren't butterflies, but there was something magical going on inside my stomach all right. Flying was absolutely, unequivocally, one of the coolest things to experience. Everything about the airline industry was exciting. Just the alluring goings-on inside the concourse itself would certainly keep me entertained.

The word *exciting* barely covers the feeling of walking out onto the tarmac in order to board our assigned jet airplane. It was very cool indeed. The tarmac was ground zero of the airport, so to speak. In those days it was common for most commercial passengers, even at international airports, to board their assigned airbus by literally walking outside onto the tarmac, negotiating other planes parked in the area to get to their designated plane. I have this memory of us walking to our plane and passing by those caterpillar caravans of luggage being pulled around by some sort of truck or tractor. I had no idea at the time what all of this meant, other than it was all new to me and way too cool. It was an awesome experience! Very cool indeed!

Of course at the larger airports these days the airliner pulls up close to the concourse, and a hood-covered extension ramp will extend out to the plane's outer door, allowing the passengers to embark from the comfortable and convenient concourse gate. This procedure is always nice and greatly appreciated when the weather outside is unfavorable, but really thought, walking around on the tarmac gives a close-up idea of how awesome these planes really are.

Of course boarding a plane is as simple a task as that of negotiating a standard stairway. Finding our assigned seats perhaps may have been a little more challenging for me at the time, but we managed all right, and I eventually was safety-belted to my seat and ready for takeoff. Takeoff didn't come immediately, though. We ended up having to sit in our seats and wait around for some important reason. I was too young to comprehend what was going on and too immature to care. Come to find out we were merely waiting for everyone to find their seats and buckle up, while the stewardess prepared everyone for takeoff.

Of course waiting for takeoff is not so simple a task for the fidgety. While most kids my age could be considered restless, I would have to say that most people considered my two brothers and me as good-natured. We had the normal high-octane energy level that most children that age exhibit, but we had been raised with a certain level of awareness. Of course fidgeting and being inquisitive as to when you're going to actually start moving is common in everyone, and most definitely in young children. My brothers and I were certainly not immune to that particularly afflictive condition. But we did have an advantage: my parents. They had prepared us for this type of scenario by teaching us time and again how to behave while out in public. It really wasn't that long of a wait.

Suddenly some colored lights flipped on. I couldn't read what the words said, since I was only four, but simultaneously the captain's voice came over the intercom system to announce our departure. So that was what those lights meant. We all listened as the captain said in a deep voice, "Welcome, ladies and gentlemen, boys and girls. This is your captain speaking. Please fasten your seat belts and prepare yourself, as we will be taking off soon." The captain sounded confident, so I knew we were in good hands.

When we actually did take off and began flying, that was when I really started to feel butterflies in my stomach. It wasn't really butterflies as much as the feeling that I had left my stomach back where we were still sitting on the tarmac. Of course those unwanted feelings didn't last long, and soon I was my old self.

From the very start, as soon as we took off from the runway, I started to become a different kid. I think the big difference was that I was quiet for the first time since being born. The way everything looked from that high up in the sky was silencing me. I just stared out the porthole and watched whatever flew by. There were so many white, fluffy, billowy clouds. They looked like large cotton balls layered on top of each other or maybe more like whipped cream or even marshmallows in hot cocoa.

Just imagine flying so high up in the air among the clouds, and it's easy to see how I was so entertained. I'm pretty sure that was the reason as to why I didn't sleep one minute while we were flying. It was rather surreal at first, but then, young minds see everything with such fascination that in no time I had lost all track of those earlier butterflies. One day I'm standing on terra firma and staring up into the sky watching all the plane flying through the clouds overhead and the next day I was actually flying through the clouds in one of those planes.

In retrospect, it's easy to understand how young minds can get so caught up in and mesmerized by the simplest of events. This is a prime example of just that, of how a young mind can see so much more than any other. Some things can be learned, and some things must absolutely be discovered.

During this travel experience, I discovered something about myself. I discovered that I had the natural gift of gab. I was indeed a loquacious little boy and that's a fact. I had never realized that about myself before, and while my parents were indeed aware of this about me, they hadn't told me.

It seems I couldn't keep from engaging in conversation with just about anyone sitting close to me. I started up these conversations with ease. I don't remember the topics we travelers talked about that day, but really, does it matter? I mean the conversations could have been about just almost anything, and I would have been happy. Finding out the truth about yourself can be a real eye-opener all in itself. I was happy with who I was and the truth about me, no doubt there. I mean, I was good at talking.

Of course, after a while, eventually the most-used question of all children's travel chants overwhelms a kid, and the words just come out as if they've been well rehearsed ... "Are we there yet?" How do all the kids everywhere in the world know this one?

There's no real attitude accompanying that question; it's just a simple question. From an early age my two brothers and I were taught that it was okay to have an opinion about something and fine to back our thoughts with passion and attitude. We were also taught that we could never show our passion or attitude with tantrums. No tantrums, period. A tantrum was an act beyond childish.

Little did I realize at the time, but soon I was about to discover and experience firsthand yet another amazing and fantastic new fact about myself. I would learn on this flight to Seattle that I could not sit still for any long-distance travel, or even short term flights for that matter. I just couldn't sit still. Period. That's all there was to it. However, on my next flight, my inability to sit still would soon get even worse.

Many years later I would of course discover that the travel time between San Francisco and Kodiak Island is relatively not that long in both distance or travel time. But try telling that to a youngster of four. That kind of news doesn't really seem to matter or make any real sense to a child who just wants to get there.

Before I really knew it, our flight captain came over the intercom and advised us that we would be landing soon. I didn't no better and assumed that we were going to be landing in Kodiak. Instead our flight plans included a planned stopover and a change of airplanes in beautiful Seattle, Washington. A stopover in Seattle, Washington, now that sounded cool. At least it held the promise for my brothers and me to be able to get out and stretch and even possibly run around for a while.

Still though, that promising news could only keep me quiet and in my seat for a short while, before I began thinking, *Come on, plane, let's land soon as we approached the Seattle International Airport - or SEA TAC which stands for Seattle, Tacoma, representing the two large communities in the area. I've always liked the name Tacoma.* It's an incredible observation to see how time is perceived through the minds of others, and acted upon, and especially children, whereby a standard thirty minutes feels a lot more like thirty days.

I also learned that day, that landing safely or otherwise at the Kodiak Island airstrip in this large jet plane would have been completely impossible because the landing strip on Kodiak was too short in runway length to accommodate such a large jet aircraft that we originally took-off in from first flight. We basically had to downsize our airplane in order to meet the challenges of landing safely at our final destination, Kodiak Island. It turns out that many things certainly are necessary and are in order for a very good reason. Landing in and changing planes in Seattle was definitely a necessary stopover with a bonus.

Speaking for the little children everywhere, let me tell the moms and dads at this time, that kids have trouble sitting still for any length of time and that doing so can be severe torture. So please be understanding of how difficult it is for them to sit still or to explain most if not all of their own behavior. While traveling by jet airplane is assuredly quicker in transportation time, fatigue can and will eventually overtake the body, and quality time-out breaks are helpful and necessary. Grown-ups and kids alike do not do well sitting still for long durations. It's a fact; motion is the lotion!

Now with that in mind, it's therefore quite understandable how and why we took advantage of the free time we had while waiting around the airport concourse for the next leg of our flight, to walk freely around the entire concourse. It turned-out to be a long enough walk for us all, and especially us kids, to move about and stretch out our highly energized young bodies—legs and arms, the whole works. After all, we had lots of energy with lots of growing parts. and though I speak of the young,

I have found that stretching is ultimately a major daily requirement for a good over-all healthy body. By the way, my mother had no problems at all keeping up with us kids, as she was pretty fit herself. She likened herself to that of a tomboy. This simple observation would soon become even more evident in the following months.

Now the idea that international airports handle airlines from other countries was fascinating in its own right. All these different airports in one area, safely delivering their passengers from one location to another location made a profound impact on my traveling experience. The gathering of all these different foreign people in one building was extremely fascinating to me. There were so many different-looking and differently dressed people in one place. Some of these travelers garments were real standouts, with some wearing brightly colored, loosely fitting clothes that made me laugh to be honest. To me they really stood out in the crowd. Some of these differently dressed people looked as though they were still wearing their pajamas.

At one point—I still remember this very well—as I was staring at a group of those differently dressed people, mesmerized by them, my mom leaned over and told me to quit staring. She said it wasn't polite. She always had good advice, and even though I wasn't really staring at these people, I kind of was. Not in the bad way though, as it was more like I was absorbing all the different nuances and aspects of life. I was very young remember and very interested as well; that's all.

I don't know exactly what it is about the airports, but for some reason, whether it was the food or all those different airplanes landing and taking off or all the differently dressed passengers from different parts of the world walking around the concourse, however this interlude sparked a certain infatuation and admiration for everything about air travel—from those people who drive around in those crazy-looking tractors to the always friendly stewardesses to the sometimes-humorous pilots and copilots. They all seemed to try to make the passengers as comfortable as possible, and they successfully succeeded. That sort of hospitality really works, and it really stuck out in my mind too.

Whichever one factor it is or whether it's the combination of everything, I have always enjoyed the aspects of air travel. It's great. Next on my list at this time was to ride the train.

Before I knew it, at some point during our newly discovered and much enjoyed people- and plane-watching obsession, the highly anticipated time for us to board our next flight arrived. Finally, at last ... *Kodiak, here we come.* And for the second time in one day we were back, flying high up in the sky once again. Yippie! No complaints from me, for by now I was not only getting used to this travel by air but was even becoming a seasoned traveler. Oh yeah!

During this flight, like the previous flight, I sat back in my seat and tried to be still. I always attempted to do my very best at whatever was asked of me, especially if we were in public. So during the beginning of this flight I was on my best behavior at every corner. Now there wasn't too much noticeable difference in this flight from our previous flight, and if they had told me the plane was smaller, which it was, I wouldn't have really noticed. The main difference was that all the people were new. It was still a jet airplane, and a jet airplane is awesome in any size. Right?

As we flew on, it was obvious that the scenery outside the plane was no different either. Once we reached the proper altitude, the captain told us over the intercom that we were in fact flying over what is known as the Alaska Panhandle and if we looked down, we might get a glimpse of the Coast Mountains through the clouds. Or maybe he said we were flying over parts of the Gulf of Alaska. Quite honestly I only caught a little bit of what he was saying and remember even less. Besides, it was during that period of the flight when I chose to hone my newly discovered gift of gab and to converse with practically every passenger that looked awake and was sitting in our seating area. Yeah, I kind of broke free for a while and started up conversations with as many of the new passengers on this new flight as I could. I just wanted to make them all feel comfortable.

But alas, I would eventually talk everyone to sleep and was eventually forced to sit in my seat and try to entertain myself for the rest of the flight. Before too long, and without much notice, I got to the point of achieving a Big Band–era, crazy-legs sort of energy. Oh yeah, Im talking improvised jazz moves. My legs had a tendency to get crazy from time to time, and this was one of those time. I stared kicking and swinging my restless legs to some sort of unrehearsed choreography that may or may not have been in sync with the sounds of music in my head. However this didn't go unnoticed, and as soon as we had landed, true to form, my mother made sure that I go apologize to the person whose seat it was that I was kicking from time to time during the flight. Of course after I apologized as only a 4 year old can do, as I graciously accepted this passengers apology for having his seat directly in the flight path of my very own leg-kicking choreography. Of course all of the adults understood what I was dealing with, but it was something I didn't know anything about, and that is that kids have a hard time sitting still for any length of time. Huh- I hadn't noticed that about myself. Of course this good natured, well seasoned air-line traveler had the good grace to put me on his level of equanimity, if for only that moment. This was a really nice lesson to learn about the proper way to approach and handle a situation. Ultimately I learned a valued lesson on how to treat people, as we left this ordeal on good terms and in an exchange of good will towards each other, we parted ways amicably. I'm taking some liberties in our exchange of decencies towards each other here. Though I do retain some memory of this incident, the blank, not so sure of areas in this memory were supported and reinforced by my other family's stories that were told regarding these same travel experiences. I wrote this part, because actually I wouldn't have understood much rancor regarding the seat-kicking incident at that time anyhow. My greatest memory of this interaction is that this man was a really nice, understanding person.

So we finally made it to Kodiak. Though it hadn't taken as long as I'd thought, we were about to land. So here we are, ready to land in beautiful Anchorage. Wait a minute … Anchorage?!

Come to find out we were going to have to stopover at another airport and switch planes yet again, only this time in beautiful Anchorage, Alaska. Apparently the second plane we downsized to was also too big to land at the Kodiak airstrip. *Just how little is Kodiak?* I wondered. No problems, though, since we kids were having a great time. In no way was any of this boring. Tiresome on our butts maybe, but certainly not boring.

This time the layover wasn't nearly as long of a wait as in the much bigger Seattle–Tacoma International Airport. The concourse in Anchorage Alaska, though quite accommodating, was certainly a much smaller than either of the two previous airports we had been. Smaller in size and not as many people either. I remember it being a much smaller is size and that they must be leaving too many doors open in that airport, because it was very obvious to me that the area was getting much cooler. That makes sense too, since we were in an area with typically much colder weather conditions. All in all, the Anchorage airport was just as efficient and interesting as the previous two airports that I had experienced that day . . . just smaller in size. Plus the excitement factor was really building up because we knew we were getting that much closer to Kodiak! Yahoo! I would like to point out, that the previous two airports had been huge in size compared to the airport in Anchorage, but all three airports held a certain fascination in their own unique ways. These airports had to have held a certain mystique, after all, they obviously left a long-lasting impression on me.

Well, once again, before I knew it, our layover at the beautiful and cool Anchorage airport was over, and before any sign of the common childish doldrums could take hold, we were ushered out to the tarmac one more time and proceeded accordingly to our assigned airplane.

I was by now a true professional when it came to boarding airplanes. I didn't need any help to board the plane, thank you very much. I may have been four years old—well, nearly four and a half—but I was confident. I knew almost exactly how to walk out to the appropriate plane, holding my mother's hand of course, and how to ascend the specialized airplane-boarding stairway—okay, with a little assistance. Allowing the stewardesses to help me find my seat and buckle me up was okay too. As I said, I was quickly becoming a pro at this travel business.

And there we went, finally, next stop Kodiak Island. I could almost hear the seagulls. Oh, and did I forget to mention that this was a propeller-type airplane, just like the ones in old period-piece movies? I did hear seagulls! And much like in the movies, this true-to-form old-school airplane had its very own large propellers connected to very large engines, with one engine and propeller attached to each wing. Perhaps as many as thirty to forty people could fit in one of these fairly modern airplanes—a fairly modern plane for the time, that is to say. This much smaller aircraft was capable of hopping from island to island, while landing safely at the many different smaller airstrips that were conveniently and strategically located throughout the entire region. This third airplane that we were flying in, was way smaller than the first two previous jet airplanes, yet come to think of it, it was just about as loud and noisy as those jet airplanes. Just as loud and capable of doing its job. In order to get a better idea of this type of plane, I suggest watching movies of that time period or, better yet, taking a trip to the local airfield.

This entire experience was all so very new to me, and my excitement level was at its highest peak, unparalleled to anything I had ever seen or been a part of . . . so far.

Airplane and Complain ... Two Different Types of Planes

Of course at my present age, I understand things much better than I did as a child. It helps to have clarity on every issue in life, and traveling is no different. I truly had no concept as to how long "not much farther" actually meant in adult terms. I tried to be patient to the best of my abilities. Im even pretty sure that at that time I may have given up on the thought shortly after I had asked the question. I even tried my best to believe that "not much farther" really meant not much farther. I may have even given up on the thought shortly after I had asked the question for the umpteenth time n went straight to grump mode. Alas, the fact still remains that for some unexplainable reason, and without much provocation on my part, the dreaded cranky travel fatigue was taking hold. Oh, it is quite contagious this travel fatigue. It can bother even grown-ups, but kids are most susceptible and almost certainly among the first to catch this crotchety behavior.

Seriously though, we had just left the Anchorage airport, and with the reassurances that Kodiak was just up ahead with perhaps no more than another 287 miles still to fly yet, and then it hit me. Out of nowhere, this incredibly powerful, persuasive force took over my body—and with complete ninja-type force, I might add. That means I didn't see it coming. Fatigue can and will get the better of any strong-willed traveler, and I was nowhere near impervious to this. My breaking point was just about to be exposed.

Gone was the gregarious child, willing to start up a conversation with any new fellow passenger. I was beginning to feel weird. I had been doing so well before, but now, not so much. I was no longer excited about traveling. Let's face it: staring at clouds, at any altitude, can lose its charm over time. *For the love of children everywhere, how much farther do we have to go before we arrive?* So go the thoughts of children everywhere who happen to be suffering from travel fatigue.

Yes indeed, those thoughts and more were most definitely going through my mind right about that time and, I might add, at a more rapid, continuous pace as time progressed. It built up more and more angst until the inevitable happened, and yes, I did it again. I asked, "Are we there yet?" That question in an uncontrollable, definitely youthful repartee. No kid means any real offense by this remark. It's merely an uncontrollable reaction due to the overwhelming fatigue.

Seriously though, my mother was really sweet, and she would simply ask us kids to sit still because we were "almost there." As if I hadn't heard that before. "Almost there" is entirely inconceivable to young children and sounds more like an eternity. My understanding of time was apparently being realized at this moment and certainly was being put to the test. It's important to note, that at this age, very few children can clearly grasp the concept of time, and I was certainly no exception to that rule. So for now, "almost there" would have to suffice.

My mother would tell us kids we were "almost there" in a soft voice that was only audible to us, and I would believe her. For the most part, I always attempted to please my parents whenever they asked something of me. For instance, during this particular flight she asked me to trust her and relax and said that in a very short amount of time we would be there. I always trusted in my parents unconditionally and always believed that they knew best. Though with all her knowledge, she had no idea what was beginning to happen to me, nor did I. What's more is that I had no idea how to express what it was that I could feel.

As time itself painfully slowed down for me during this flight, those loving and sympathetic words from my mother began to lose their power of persuasion. As much fun as this flying business was, the only thing I wanted at that particular point in time was for the plane to land, anywhere would do, so I could get out and run. Ahhhh! I could not understand this weird feeling and why it was beginning to feel more and more crazy weird, like it was gaining on me and I couldn't run away.

These symptoms of stiffness and discomfort were taking their toll on other people as well. I know it wasn't just me feeling uncomfortable, because I saw other passengers acting restless and stretching in their seats too. And suddenly, voilà, just like that those familiar lights flashed, those lights that must have spelled out something important like "We're here," because once again, as soon as those lights lit up, all the passengers began fastening their seat belts. I couldn't read yet, but through observation, this being my third plane flight in just one day, I was beginning to take notice.

Hurry please, we need to land quickly, I thought. I really couldn't wait any longer. What was the holdup anyway? There was no real holdup, not really; landing just takes a little time and patience. Once again, try telling that to a child, especially a child who is acting funny, one who is painfully experiencing an abundance of that bottled-up youthful energy that just has to be released periodically. It's extremely difficult to be patient when we're young, compounded by not having a clear understanding of most things going on around us or with us.

As Kodiak Island came into view, I was able to take my mind off of the dreaded body aches for a much appreciated brief moment, by looking out the porthole and glimpsing parts of the island. At first glance I mostly saw water. *Hey, there's only water down there! Water, water everywhere,* I thought. Again … mostly confusion. It was amazing to see all that water down below, but at the same time it was also a bit disconcerting. Remembering that I had just moved away from a very large valley in California where there was plenty of open land, and to see nothing but water at first glance was a bit confusing. I understand, it was clearly a water world we were moving to.

Come to find out, we were flying over an area of the Gulf of Alaska, which is indeed a very large area of open water. No wonder I was having so much trouble spotting Kodiak Island.

KNOW WHEN IT'S TIME TO LEAVE

Cool, we had safely landed and now we can disembark from our airbus. Of course immediately upon our safe landing, and with the go ahead from the stewardess the other passengers began to leave their seats and off from the plane. I too was attempting to do so, but there was just one problem. That funny feeling I had been experiencing earlier was back. This funny feeling was one of those unexplainable, first-time-experience conundrums. Just what in the world was my body trying to tell me? As soon as I went to get up out of my seat, I noticed this all-over-my-body tingling sensation. My butt felt the worst, kind of flattened out. And my legs … what legs? I had no legs, at least none that were in working order anyway.

As soon as I tried to stand up, I felt a weird, tingling sensation in my legs and feet. The little needles tingling in my legs made it extremely difficult to walk. Even though this brand-new feeling was unwanted, I couldn't keep from exploding into that kind of laughter like a wounded giggle. What the?! Every time I took another step forward, I felt this overwhelming tickling in my legs and feet that caused me to giggle uncontrollably. And I wasn't the kind of kid to just start giggling, or was I?

I was, for the first time in my very young life—as far as I can remember anyway—suffering from the dreaded sleeping-legs syndrome. My mother, as well as some of the other concerned passengers, attempted to explain to me that my legs had fallen asleep during the long flight.

Here I was, the whole entire trip, entirely way too excited and anxious to even think about sleeping, and next thing I know, my legs and feet had nodded off instead.

I could barely walk off the plane under my own navigational skills without giggling rather hysterically. People gave me looks that seemed to say, "What's wrong with that child?"

I loved everything I learned about flying that day, but let's face it: when it comes to very young children with all that natural energy, requiring them to sit still for several hours at a time makes about as much sense as trying to convince them that you're "almost there."

ISLAND OF THE MIDNIGHT SUN

Kodiak Island is an island approximately fifty miles wide and one hundred miles long. It parallels the beautiful Alaska Peninsula, separated only by the deep, cold waters of the Shelikof Strait, which is 30 miles wide and 130 miles long. Along the other borders of Kodiak Island are the waters of the Gulf of Alaska and the Pacific Ocean. Kodiak Island is comprised of one large major portion of land along with several smaller islets with their own individual and unique beaches.

During those days, Kodiak Island was home to the brave men and women stationed at the US naval station, which, by the way, was where our plane landed. During this time it was called US Naval Station Kodiak Alaska, however it was renamed in 1964 to Coast Guard Air Station Kodiak. The station is home to some of the bravest men and women who serve the public and continuously display their high standards of professionalism while performing their humanitarian duties. The men and woman that serve at the Kodiak coast guard outpost are a great asset throughout the region, saving many lives each year through their heroic yet dutiful tasks. No man or woman is an island!

Conveniently our plane landed at the Us Naval Station outpost where it was just a few miles away by car from the town of Kodiak. Plus it was the hub where all major air traffic at the time was handled, including all commercial airlines on the island. In other words, it was the only airport in the area at the time to handle this type of air traffic.

So it turned out that our new hometown of Kodiak wasn't so isolated and out of touch with the outside world after all. I also noticed that there was a lot more land space than I originally thought when I first saw Kodiak Island from our planes port hole. This island wasn't cut off from the world; it had connections, so to speak, major connections. The town of Kodiak is located on the southeast region of the island, where it has the distinct privilege of enjoyable ocean sea breezes and many spectacular scenic views of this island with its many beautiful sheltered coves.

Now it was in these areas that several of the island's inhabitants resided. Several of these residents had ownership of their own personal floatplanes, so called because of the tandem pontoons that straddle the undercarriage so that the planes can land, float, and take off on open water. These small aircraft were fairly abundant in the area due to the high demand of their extreme usefulness and ability to land safely in small isolated islet coves while delivering needed supplies to someone in need. Very necessary for an areas such as these islets and coastal towns were, as these floatplanes are relied upon as delivery planes, ferrying necessary supplies to areas that have only water-requiring capabilities.

I have found that it is extremely helpful to get the complete understanding of a certain situation from the actual people involved. Therefore, in this case it's probably easier to understand the importance and need of small aircraft in this area from the local people's perspective, those in need of those supplies. For all practical reasons, each and every one of these seaplanes was highly important for the welfare and success of the inhabitants in this region. The supply routes that they served were direct proof of their importance to the areas strength. From my youthful perspective, however, watching these floatplanes take off and land on water was one of the coolest thing to do to pass the time. From large aircraft all the way down to the very smallest of aircraft, many were busy with constantly resupplying the various hamlets throughout the inhabited islets as well as providing delivery services throughout this vast geographical location.

Large or small, everyone is important and has a proper place, as no man is an island ... The same goes for a successful network of islands too. No one stands alone.

KODIAK IS A VERY COOL PLACE

Alaska, Kodiak Island in particular, was only a few hundred miles by land or by sea from the beautiful, iconic cities of San Francisco and Oakland in California. While the travel time between San Francisco and Kodiak took many hours, we still managed to complete our trip from sunny California to cool Kodiak Island all during the daylight hours. It may not be that long in travel distance and may not take that long in travel time, but for us kids traveling all day seemed to take forever. Kids everywhere can pack a lot of excitement into just one day, and that makes it seem like a lot longer of a travel experience.

It was late afternoon when we all got our first glimpse of Kodiak Island. Just uttering *Kodiak Island* to me at that time would make me instantly conjure up excitement about the potential new adventures in an unfamiliar place that I would soon be calling my home. Now after landing and being successfully ushered off the plane—without any more incidents, I might add—we hastily scooted off the tarmac, hurriedly passing right on through the even tinier airport terminal and out to the parking lot to meet up with my dad. My dad had contractual obligations to his employers to show up for his job on time, so he had left for Kodiak three days earlier.

Once we met up with my dad just outside the airport terminal, I was able to get a quick read on my new surroundings. Kodiak Island was absolutely intriguing to say the least. As soon as we'd gotten off the plane, I had realized that this new place was entirely different in appearance from California. Evergreen trees seemed to be growing everywhere, especially on the nearby foothills, which by the way were surprisingly very close in relative distance.

Another significant thing I remember upon our arrival was that practically every single one of my extremely youthful, unchallenged, inexperienced senses were all on high alert. The many different smells floating in the late-evening air were way different from anything I was used to smelling back in California. And the various new sounds of unknown origins were ... Well, let's just say I had no idea where these sounds were coming from, let alone what could possibly be making them. Whoa! I mean there was a good chance those sounds were coming from the same creatures from my uncles' stories. I mean, come on, just what kind of an animal can even make those kinds of noises? Maybe it was the abominable snowman spoken of in those stories I had been told. I remember in the story he did a lot of screaming which seemed to scare a lot of people. Well actually, it turns out that most of those noises were emanating from the Kodiak Harbor, as well as the local seafood enterprises. But what a noise . . . and what an imagination.

Another thing of importance was that after stepping off the plane, we were all in agreement that the weather was very different from what it had been like earlier in the day. Chilly to say the least! Every one of us was feeling the chill and for a very good reason too. In the summer Kodiak Island and San Francisco both have coastal breezes with a mix of foggy and sunny days. The main difference is the temperature. For example, in the days leading up to our departure at the end of August, the city we left behind was enjoying nice warm temperatures in the upper eighties to low nineties. And when we landed on the island, it was only in the upper fifties. *Big* difference. *Biiiig* difference.

All the same though, no one really seemed to mind the cooler weather. At least we didn't seem to mind, and eventually considered it to be nice, pleasant weather to live in ... especially once we all were dressed appropriately for the weather conditions. Let me point out that this area's indigenous people, the Alutiiq tribe, designed their own handmade clothing specifically for staying dry during the wet, rainy months. All in all, this island had a completely tolerable chill to it. I wouldn't want to give the impression that this place was cold. Kodiak Island's chill wasn't uncomfortable, but it was still evident to newcomers. It was the type of cooling chill that said, "Hello, welcome to Kodiak Island" and "Never forget; always remember-brr-brr-brr, that Kodiak is a cool place." At least that's the way I remember it. And had I been thinking clearly at that time, I might have very well deduced that that was exactly what I had heard off in the distance after I'd first stepped off the plane at the Kodiak airport.

Of course I'm being a little facetious about that part. Actually, Kodiak Island doesn't experience extreme weather conditions like those found on the mainland of Alaska. In truth, the weather conditions on Kodiak Island are quite tolerable year-round. Moreover, the whole entire time we spent on the island, the varying weather conditions never seemed to bother any one of us at all, especially after we all got acclimated to the new environment.

Lesson learned, after living in an area for a while, most people, if not all, will acclimate themselves to their surroundings. We were no different as we acclimated quite quickly to every new and different nuance of living in a new area of the world.

In all fairness, Kodiak Island can and does get much warmer during the summer. Not all of Alaska is cold like some movies depict. Yes indeed, Kodiak Island has very enjoyable and warm summer weather.

ROAD TESTED, ROAD AND FAMILY APPROVED

As I pointed out, my dad had traveled on up to Kodiak Island a couple of days ahead of us. Part of the reason he did so was to secure our new house as well as to take our dog, Lizzie, with him. He also needed to secure a vehicle for us all to travel and roam about the island. Of course this car was going to be used for more than just trivial island hopping. Oh no, my dad had plans of commuting to work in this new car and ferrying us all around the area. I had been told early on that as soon as we got to the island, we were going to have a new family car to ride around in.

I must admit that once again in my life I was rather excited about seeing something brand new. And this car was new, and … where was it? Wait, there it was, sitting in the parking lot almost completely hidden by the other bigger cars. This was going to be the car that would take us pretty much wherever we needed to go during our sojourn on this island? What a great car it turned out to be too—eventually. Not at first, though; at first it looked like it didn't belong in this rough area.

It was so small compared to all the other larger cars and four-wheel-drive trucks that were sharing the same parking lot. It was a 1958 Renault, a French-made car. This car was truly small, way smaller than the car we'd left back in California. It was shaped like a bubble and about the same size of its contemporary the VW Beetle. It was by no means large and cumbersome like all the other much bigger cars and was far less cool looking than the four-wheel-drive pickup trucks sitting along side it. And of course, this was in no way the era for economical compact cars. Small cars may have been very popular in European countries at the time but not so much in the United States. It was quite a rare sight for us kids to even see one of those little economy cars when we lived back in California, much less see a little European car up close, and now we had the opportunity to climb into one for the first time.

And climb inside we did.

Youngster or not, even I could recognize and appreciate the complexities involving a family of five, two adults and three young boys, plus one large German shepherd successfully climbing into something of this diminutive size. Allow me to clarify this image here with some insider perspective. My dad was six foot two and weighed around 235 pounds, and this car wasn't much bigger than one of those clown cars used in circus acts.

Just the same, we all managed to successfully pile into this little eco-friendly car without any problems other than the seating arrangement. I wanted a window seat, and so did my two older brothers. There's really no need to say who got the middle seat without a window. Look, it's tough being short, and being that short while sitting in the backseat of a very small car unable to see out very far in any direction is frustrating—tolerable but frustrating.

And as far as those unknown smells my brother Tim and I had detected earlier, well, those turned out to be no more than that which comes from a new location. Okay, so that alluring odor was from the fish canneries in the area. New smells take time to get used to, and this one was definitely going to take some time to get used to.

So as our daylong travel to Kodiak Island came to an end, so too concluded the course of daylight itself, turning into twilight as the sun set behind the foothills, rapidly transforming the sky into dusk as we drove away from the small Kodiak airport, heading toward our new home and the undiscovered adventures awaiting me.

LESSONS IN LIFE AND BOUNDARIES

Stepping down onto new and unfamiliar terra firma was no different than stepping onto the first of the series of planes that brought us to Kodiak Island in the first place. But Kodiak Island itself? Just the mention of Kodiak can give me a chill, the good kind of chill, the kind of happy chill that brings on goose bumps and evokes really good thoughts and memories. At the time of our arrival on Kodiak Island I of course had no memories to recall upon yet; however, that particular dilemma would soon be remedied, as I was about to embark on many different childhood explorations. Adventures are where childhood memories come from, and I was eager to start making some serious memories. Looking back, I can say I had clearly made a few long-lasting memories just by traveling to Kodiak Island.

From the very first moment of our arrival, we all began learning a whole new way of life. The whole concept of going from living in the city/agronomy lifestyle to this small island-village and harbor-town lifestyle was, to say the least, an adventure of a lifetime.

First things first, my parents taught us the fundamentals of staying safe in the new surroundings, and that meant we kids had to understand that there were lots of wild animals living close by, including the mighty Kodiak brown bear, which lived and roamed certain areas of the island. Therefore, it was highly imperative that I learn early on not only how important it is to keep a sharp lookout for any possible danger, but also how to identify all the various avenues from which danger can approach. It's an age-old lesson regarding life and survival and how to stay that way … healthy and alive!

I confidently attest to the importance of staying alert. Learning this highly important lesson early in life has been extremely useful to me.

Kids Will Be Kids, and
Bears Will Be Bears

Most young children will follow others, and following older brothers and sisters is certainly nothing new. Older siblings always lead the younger ones; that's just how it goes. I was certainly no different when it came to my relationship with my two older brothers, Tim and Fitzo. Of course I was going to follow their lead, because being older meant that they had a better idea about certain things.

Anytime we kids were reminded that bears were freely roaming around the island—which, by the way, automatically and instantly upped the awesome factor—my oldest brother, Fitzo, would make some sort of noise. So I too made the same noise. I mean I was just going along with whatever either of my two older brothers said. Bears? Cool! I mean, how cool is that? If my brothers said it was cool, then it was. My brothers didn't act scared, so I wasn't about to either. I didn't even know what a bear looked like, but didn't they sound cool? Of course we were never in any real danger, and while bears weren't entirely a big threat to the townspeople, it was always a good idea to keep a sharp eye out for any stray or unintimidated hungry bear foraging for food.

One time my mother, my brother Tim, Lizzie, and I were out for a country drive or perhaps coming back from the beach, and we stopped and got out to do a little berry picking close to the road. While we were picking, my mother saw a bear, very close to us too! She quickly and quietly ushered us kids and Lizzie back into the car, and off we drove down the hill, speeding in that little car of ours, hoping the bear didn't see us a tiny little berry getting away by rolling down the hill. I didn't see the bear, but my mother sure did. That was pretty obvious by the way she drove out of there, with all of us inside the car wondering just how fast this car could go … Heading downhill that little car could flat out move!

THE ONLY ACCEPTABLE TYPE OF NAME-CALLING

Now even though the town of Kodiak was rather small in comparison to our previous hometown back in California, it was still considered the metropolitan town of the island in comparison to some of the other nearby towns, which had really cool names like Akhiak, Karluk, Uyak, and of course the much-easier-to-pronounce Seal's Cove. The very quaint town of Kodiak was the biggest village on the entire island. And what's more, the town of Kodiak had some history; it was the oldest established nonnative commercial-fishing village.

Many people often referred to Kodiak Island as simply "the Green Island." Not that many years earlier Kodiak Island had been labeled the "Emerald Island" because of its lush, tall green grass. Of course it's not *the* Emerald Island. That prestigious distinction goes to the great country of Ireland, which is also an island, a much larger island than Kodiak Island albeit but an island all the same. Just one glance at Kodiak Island, whether from on a boat far out on the ocean waters or from a vantage point high in the air, makes its two nicknames completely understandable.

Adding to the beauty of the islands lush green hillsides, and lovely green appearance are the indigenous conifers growing freely throughout the entire area. In fact there were many small forested type patches of tall evergreen conifers and local deciduous underbrush sharing these hills. Obviously these grass-covered hillsides were watered and well taken care of and supported by the frequented humid Pacific Ocean breezes. I love those types of ocean breezes. Naturally I learned that these mist filled ocean breezes were in fact very important to the area, as well as helping to nourish the tall grass, it benefited the tall conifers of the area as well as every living creature receiving life in this immediate ecosystem. It was an obvious lesson in how natural occurrences can and will encourage others to grow tall.

GETTING TERRA FAMILIAR

Now it just so happens that one of the coolest-looking and most mysterious of these bands of evergreen forests ran the ridge-top just up the hill from our house. Our home had a decent size front yard and a nice big backyard. More on both of those later.

Kodiak Harbor was located down the hill from and in eyesight of our house. It's interesting to note that this little harbor town has a long history with the fishing industry, which explains the nearly continuous whiffs of something very unflattering wafted through the local fishing village. It didn't take long to realize that with the seafood processing plants, which were built right along the shores of the local harbor system, came the strong odor of fish and bound to be present everywhere. It was the type of smell that I thought at first I would probably never get used to, and yet, in no time at all I had forgotten about it. Didn't really smell it as so strong and offensive that is too say. Famous for it's long history, this old fishing town has long held the prestigious distinction for being one of the main hubs of the Alaskan fishing fleet.

The Kodiak harbor system is uniquely protected by a series of conveniently located islets that form a protective breakwater and provide safety from the strong and harsh forces of nature via the Gulf of Alaska and the mighty Pacific Ocean itself, which is by the way, the largest ocean in the world, I might add.

I was too young to remember much prior to our moving to beautiful Kodiak Island, but I do remember forming a pretty good bond with this island from the very start, and my adventures were only just beginning. It didn't take long for me to feel this way about my new island home, and everyone in my family looked very happy to be here as well. That's why it takes no stretch of the imagination to see why Kodiak Island was such a cool place to be a part of, and it just kept getting better for me, day after day..

Yes, of course there was a certain danger level, but that can be said of any place. It certainly was highly important to my parents to repetitively reiterate to us kids how important it was to be more aware of our surroundings and those around us. Part of keeping us safe included specifying just how far from the house we could go to play. My parents were the ones to decide exactly where our boundaries were. If I had my choice, I would just play on. My parents really didn't have to tell me but maybe once or twice where I could or could not play. I remember my parents reminding me of my boundaries on a few occasions and of course being reminded was important in helping me to remember.

I think I was always more confused when one of my parents would catch up to me after I wandered off and ask, "What did I say about wandering off?" My ready-made answer was "To not to?" or maybe just stare at the ground for a bit, until they asked me again. Eventually either one of my parents or both would follow up that first question with the even more worse "What did I tell you?" I mean, how does a kid answer that one? Which time were they referring to? By this time in my life I'd already been told a lot of things. To which time would they be referring?

My personal boundaries were not just confined to my front-yard and backyard playgrounds but also included the boundaries I took with me whenever we were in town, meaning the boundaries of how I was expected to behave. I was expected to be on my best behavior at all times and especially whenever we were in public. And we were about to trek down into town for the first time. We were going to learn the necessary layout of the extended area by taking a nature hike through the neighborhood which included an informative stroll into town. With such a small neighborhood it didn't take long before we found a commonly used public trail that had just the right number of switchbacks so we could easily traverse the gentle downhill slope. This seemingly popular hiking trail was landscaped on both sides with the perfect combination of lovely wildflowers and wild berries, as well as the occasional limited cluster of tall conifers spotted occasionally as the hikers traverse the trail.

This trail led us right to the outskirts of town, and basically right onto the streets. It didn't seem like that long of a walk, and I mean just like that, we were walking down one of the streets of Kodiak town. Now from a small child's perspective, this little town looked like and had the feel of one of those quaint little fishing villages from a postcard, with a small boat harbor accompanied with that patina-looking boardwalk. It truly was a small and quiet town in comparison to our last hometown. This town had a sort of old-fashioned feel to it; that was very obvious right from the beginning. A cozy, comfortable feel. Oh I know now, there isn't any traffic to speak of. I mean they have streets, and cars to drive on these streets, it's just not that occupied with cars, that's all.

It's important to point-out at this time, that this town, though small in size, and on an island no less, had most all of the essentials that big cities have, only downsized of course—things like a bank, post office, grocery store, barbershop, and the ever-so-popular and absolutely necessary bowling alley. Everybody in my family loved bowling, so this made our new hometown that much more homey.

Bowling is a fun sport that just about everyone can participate in, whether a person is good at it or not. Plus it was pretty much a given that up to that point I was considered clumsy, and bowling was the only sport I could truly be a part of without getting into too much trouble. I don't believe I threw objects very well or with any proficient accuracy at this age, so horseshoes was certainly out of the question for me, but while I lacked in throwing, I made up for it by being superb at rolling large bowling balls down a wooden lane.

This town truly was well supplied which included the all-important hunting supply store and of course a full and complete fishing tackle shop. I think those two stores were always busy and always open. Well, at least they were always busy with customers every time we went by. Yeah, I wonder why?

I cannot attest to how it is on the island today, but back in those days, the roads on the island were paved differently than they were back in California. There were no blacktop or asphalt roads anywhere to be found, yet we drove on roads that looked like all other well-paved roads. It turns out that history had a bigger part to play in the construction of the roads on the island, as they had been built several years earlier by mixing a road pavement batch that included volcanic ash. Yup, that's right, volcanic ash.

At one time, this volcanic ash was in such abundance that a thick layer of it covered everything in sight over the entire island. The nice turn of affairs here is that it turns out that the ash from the local volcanos could be used as an important part of forming favorable road conditions. This huge amount of ash was the result of the 1912 volcanic eruption of Mount Katmai, which is located less than a couple hundred miles away across the Shelikof Strait on the interior of the Alaska Peninsula. This regional area of the Alaska Peninsula is known as the Valley of Ten Thousand Smokes.

The lessons we kids learned while familiarizing ourselves with the area would not have been complete had we not been familiarized with all things possible and not just those around our own home. This would include just about everything we saw everywhere we went.

The location of our local school in correlation to our home played an important part in our daily hikes. This school was conveniently located just a couple of blocks down the street from our house, and better yet, our new favorite hiking trail, the one that led down into town, began its descent close to the school grounds. As I remember, the Kodiak school system operated out of one large building that accommodated the entire academic school grades.

If this is true, then the Kodiak educational system welcomed kindergarten children just starting out on their own quests toward higher education and at the same time were preparing to say good-bye to the senior-grade high schoolers who were adjusting to their final year of their public school education. Obviously at four years of age I was too young to attend school, yet I was once again reminded it would be but a short time before I would be old enough.

PUSHING THOSE BOUNDARIES

I had quickly come to realize that this little island had its own unique differences from city life all right. It had no backyard fence what so ever, and our house just happened to be a corner lot, with no fence on either side of the house either. With the endless suggestion of open space to go explore, it's no wonder I had a propensity to wander with little slow-moving creeks nearby inciting me to play. The freedom to go outdoors though came with a condition. This condition was that before I was allowed to go outside and play on my own, I had to first listen to my mother recite the familiar daily warning about playing outside by myself. Understanding that not necessarily all the outdoors was safe for me to just go hang around and play. I had to abide by my parents' rules, or else I didn't get to be outside. My parents wanted me and my brothers to understand that only a certain smaller portion of the area within the immediate vicinity of our home was ours to explore, and not to start wandering off.

I was an adventurous four-year-old and innocently disobeyed my limited play area on a few occasions. When it all comes down to it, this precaution was for my own safety, and I would learn to understand this eventually. Personally I had no real opinion one way or the other about where I was permitted to play in the first place—absolutely no real opinion at all, not one whatsoever … yeah right. I mean, the whole entire area looked the same to me. Boundary lines are easily overlooked when children are having innocent fun, and so ultimately at some point my parents began explicitly forbidding me in the areas they deemed off limits. Of course my brother Tim had found these really cool places to go play just up the street from our house and I wanted to go too. The layout of the street our house was on continued on up past our home for another block and a half and then quickly stopped at the base of the nearby hillside. This hillside was covered with conifers that formed an ominous-looking forest hilltop. These evergreen trees grew clear down the side of that hillside right up nearly where our street ended. It was an extremely ominous-looking forested hillside to me; plus it also happened to be one of those areas that garnered the off-limits distinction.

And if the beckoning of the mountain wasn't enough by itself to lure me out past my prearranged boundary lines, then the cool-looking earthmover's sitting at the base of this hillside sure were. Oh, my parents told us kids not to play on the equipment, but we figured that if we could climb up, then we could play. Yeah, I stayed away from all the cool-looking heavy equipment machinery for about as long as it takes for an older brother to say, "Come on, let's go!" Of course there where consequences to pay for not following the rules. And I payed alright.

Now obviously some areas were emphatically off limits to me and for very good reasons. These particular areas of main concern were based on the danger level they presented to me at this young age. And of course there was that one place in the area that was completely off limits to me, and this forbidden zone just happened to be the ominous-looking forested hillside that, in my eyes, was only a short hop skip and a jump down the street from our house. This hillside trailed up over the top, continuing on up to an even denser forest that kept continuing on until those trees caught up to a yet an even denser patch of forest that went to … well, I don't know where it went, because I wasn't allowed up there. But I was told all about it by my brother Tim who said that on one occasion our older brother Fitzo took him on up over that hill quite a distance. As a matter of fact, Tim told me that they hiked as far as the bottom of the other side of the forested hill where it opened up onto a long running beach where they discovered an old derelict ship. It was of course emphatically expressed that I not go up that forest trail, or anywhere near it for that matter. I wonder if my dad ever knew my older brothers were.

It's important to understand that for most people remembering—whether it's just a simple word, for example, or a common act like tying one's own shoes—takes practice and repetition. So too did remembering my boundaries take practice. My parents emphasized where we kids were allowed to play more than once. I know I sure got reminded a lot.

I was often reminded of my limits, especially after being caught playing in the areas I had been previously warned about, like playing along while following i the creek further down the hillside than was deemed safe. When my brothers and I did break the rules, my parents often voiced their disapproval and reprimanded us. True to form, they repeated their concerns about me playing in the creek so far from the house. And if any of us kids were in the same room or in earshot of the admonishment we were getting, then the others too, whether they had been involved or not, would receive the same message from my parents merely as a supplemental. Not only were we kids expected to understand and obey these guidelines my parents were attempting to purvey, but we were also expected to fulfill their parental proclamations through our own everyday actions.

Everything worthwhile takes time and patience, and therefore patience is definitely a healthy virtue to hold on to.

As I previously said, I was content with the large area of freedom that was given to me to explore, but I seemed to have a need to explore a little more. I was so young and had so much to learn yet.

For instance, I was drawn to the nearby hillside with its mysterious groves of thick evergreens that created a darkened forest floor where shadows even had shadows. Even to this day I can remember how ominous yet somehow subtlety inviting that forested hillside was to me. I really don't know how I resisted any further investigation on my part ... but I did. Perhaps a great deal of my self-control came by way of my brother Tim. Ah, the wisdom of elders.

My parents always saw to it that we kids learned as much as we could about the important issues like safety, and because this was a new neighborhood, we were taught as many specifics regarding the area as we could before heading out the front door. My parents stressed the fact that though it would be fairly unusual to see any dangerous wild animals roaming around our community or nearby town, these wild animals were still a possible threat to our safety and could be in our area on any given day and at any time of day. If this were ever to occur, we were instructed to make fast for the front door.

My parents also gave me plenty of warnings that if I were to wander off too far, I just might not remember how to get back safely to our new home. This of course went for Lizzie too. Lizzie and I actually shared the exact same boundaries. And just like us kids, Lizzie also needed to learn where her boundary lines were. Merely walking her around our new home a few times while pausing now and then to let her mark her area was about all she needed to confirm this. Everyone knows that dogs can smell way better than us humans can, so this little land marking she did gave her pretty much all the information she would ever need. No more using the neighbors' yards as a bathroom. Right!

Whenever people are in the wilds of nature, certain appropriate mannerisms will help keep them safe. It's not wise or advised to drop your guard when out and about in the wilds of nature, or anywhere else for that matter. My parents insisted we learn and memorize that system.

Know the park rules! Absolutely everywhere anyone sojourns there are new procedures and rules to observe and dangers of all sorts. These important rules were certainly observed by all of us kids, including the neighbor kids, who all seemed to be well informed of this practice by the time we moved there.

Our new home was located in what I would consider a near-perfect area that added to its entertainment value. We had a small grove of maybe twelve or 14 tall evergreen trees in our backyard, which meant hours of unlimited fun with just our imagination. We had one of the coolest backyard playgrounds, complete with our very own creek that flowed alongside and around our house down the sloping hillside of our backyard and on down the hillside flowing down eventually pouring into the ocean.

I was absolutely convinced from the very beginning that this creek went somewhere fascinating. My curiosity got the better of me on more than one occasion, and I believe it was my curiosity and imagination for more adventures and answers to my questions that led me to follow the creek farther down the hill than I was allowed. That desire to stretch my boundaries just a little bit was out of functioning curiosity rather than out of conscious disrespect. It has to be understood that this slow-flowing creek meandered past our house and through part of our small forest, steadily down the hill in the general direction of our new home town of Kodiak. This creek in particular was very small in size and the volume of water that flowed certainly not enough to float myself in, however, this diminutive creek held a powerful influence on me, like that of the much bigger Russian River located only few miles away. This simple creek captivated my imagination early on, to the point where I would certainly have to satisfy my curiosity by finding out just where all those floating things I'd sent down the creek—all at different times of course—had actually ended up.

It's a great feeling of satisfaction to find the end results to an action. Maybe the results are not entirely the way we want, but nonetheless, just the knowledge of the results can be very rewarding to some. The satisfactory end result here is that, as we all know, if free-flowing water isn't dammed up somewhere down the line, it will eventually follow the path with the least resistance to the bottom of the headlands and eventually join the bay waters. I did not know that then. After all, I was always caught long before I got close to the ocean. But I think I wanted to find the answer to my question, which was, Where does this creek end up?

FAST FOODS

I was learning a subtle yet ongoing lesson in the world of food from the time I was able to eat solid food. This daily lesson was continuously brought to my attention without much fanfare. This particular lesson could be referred to as a silent lesson since three times a day my mother would cook our meals without getting a great deal of outwardly spoken gratitude.

Every morning at my house we would sit at the table and start our day off the right way with some sort of really good, healthy breakfast that might be vastly different from the previous morning's. We always had something different every morning for breakfast in order to start each day off right. Our lunches were always prepared in the same manner with TLC and always something a little different from the day before. Balance. And by the time dinnertime came around, she was back in the kitchen preparing us a nutritious evening meal. All these meals were specifically planned out by what my mother had previously decided. It didn't seem to take her that much time to plan these dinners really, but it was her time, and she did it well.

It turns out that my mother was planning our meals and feeding us all these great tasting healthy, nutritious meals with complete understanding of the importance of various sources of nutrition for growing children as well as adults. That's something all special moms and dads adhere to, especially while raising young children.

My brothers and I were raised to always try to show our gratitude for our meals by thanking my mom after we ate. It was always just a simple "Thanks, Mom." Those types of courtesies were part of the manners lesson. I know she sure appreciated our gratitude for her effort.

However, eating absolutely everything on my plate was the ultimate sign to my mom that the food was all right and very much appreciated. Starting from the very beginning of my solid-food eating experience, practically every meal we ate was at home, and almost every meal was entirely cooked and prepared by my mom or occasionally my dad. Not only were nearly all our meals homemade, but they were all uniquely different from the previous day's. Mom always changed the food menu from day to day in order to give our bodies a chance to work out the problems or issues they might have with some particular food. This way fatty foods don't have as good a chance to build up in the body as fast. Another advantage was that we got that many more chances to eat that many more different good-tasting, nutritious foods. This and the fact that we all ate well-balanced meals helped us kids to grow up strong and healthy, giving us the added advantage of being better able to fight off medical issues. Look it up.

The worst part—if you could call any of it bad—was that while we lived on Kodiak Island, we pretty much had to eat canned vegetables. Yuck, especially beets. Seriously! Beets and canned spinach. How dare anybody try to feed kids certain types of vegetables and try to call them food, let alone canned veggies. Ugh! Whatever my mother chose to be our veggie for that particular nights dinner, we were expected to eat it. All of it too! "Clean your plate because those vegetables are good for you. Some children in other countries don't have it so well," my mother would say to us kids practically every time we petitioned to skip the healthy food.

However, I did like some vegetables. Carrots and corn were my favorite, and I never had any problem eating those vegetables. Freshly picked, or right out of the can, carrots and corn were fine by me. But those beets, and that spinach, oh my gosh, well, they're not really vegetables now are they? And if it doesn't stay down, then it isn't really food and can't be called eating. I'm grateful we never had both beets and spinach served to us on the same dinner plate. I don't believe I would have ever survived that combination.

My mom was old school and very adamant that we kids learn and thoroughly understood the importance of eating a well-balanced meal that included vegetables. She was especially adamant about this well-balanced-meal idea of hers while, as she would put it, "the body is young and developing." Remember, repetition works. Obviously my mother was very patient and would explain that it's important to eat well during every stage of life. It was put to us kids, that while the body is growing and developing, it needs plenty of good nutritious foods from lots of different sources. i.e. fruits and vegetables.

This simple explanation of hers seemed plausible, which in turn seemed to help me swallow those undesirable vegetables with less negative reactions, especially when I saw my parents eat those very same vegetables. But when it came to certain vegetables, well, some were good, and some were horrible. I figured that those nasty-tasting vegetables grew in the dirt and that was why they tasted so bad. It was hard for me at the time to wrap my head around the idea that something that tasted so bad could actually be very good for my health and that I should eat as many fruits and vegetables as possible whether I liked them or not. Quite the mental conundrum.

I loved my parents very much, and I just knew to trust them because they were wise and knew how to take care of me. Up to this point, that is. I don't really remember how I reacted toward vegetables in my first three years of my life, but by four years of age I remember us kids getting very creative and trying to hide our spinach in some mashed potatoes, swirling it in a thin layer over our plates so as to mask the fact that we had actually eaten very little. We thought it looked legitimate. Sometimes we tried hiding those small cubed chunks of red beets under the raised-up edges of our square dinner plates. They hid very well under there until the plates were taken from the table, exposing our childish attempts of deceit. But our tricks seemed to work for us the first few times we tried to deceive our mother this way. However, eventually she called us on it, and from that point on, we were not going to get away with misbehaving, or playing with our food that way any longer. The rule was we had to eat all the food on our plates, including all vegetables, in order to be excused from the table and allowed to watch television. FYI, black-and-white television with rabbit ears for improved reception was what we looked forward to watching T.V. on. I seem to remember missing a lot of family-time television, as I also remember that sometimes, some dinners just simply required the use of extra napkins.

Basically I chalk this up as an easy lesson to learn, and it goes pretty much like this: try to eat good foods so you can feel good too. To stay healthy and feeling good we must eat good foods. Practice a healthy lifestyle by eating more and different varieties of fruits and vegetables and by cooking 95 percent of meals at home if possible.

Life has constant lessons to be learned while acted upon, and my mother always made an honest effort to teach us these simple yet often overlooked principles. Thanks, Mom and Dad, good lesson!

AHHH! SOFT WHITE FLAKES OF _ _ _ _ ?

Having come from a large open-range valley region in Northern California, where the snow was found only in the higher elevations, for me seeing snow for the first time was an experience full of complete wonder. Snow? I knew what rain was, but snow?

I may have been introduced to the snow back when we were living in California. I mean it's possible that I reacted differently at the age of two or three. I really can't exactly remember any of the particulars of that first day, not definitively, other than knowing that for the first time I was seeing snowfall and having a great time trying to catch the small snowflakes in my mouth as snowflakes landed on my face almost instantly melting from the heat of my flushed face. I had no idea what this stuff was or where it was coming from … other then from the sky that is. Before long, and in no-time at all, enough snow had accumulated for the fun times to really begin. So many different ways to have fun with snow and so many different and exciting snow days were coming my way.

I think it's necessary to point out that not one of us ever truly suffered from the cold weather while living on the island, and that's because shortly after we arrived, my mom got busy making sure that all of us were outfitted to meet that Kodiak Island dress code. Okay, perhaps we were outfitted in simple, ordinary, albeit cozy and warm store-bought boots and not authentic mukluks, but we paid close attention to the locals and learned from them how to dress as best we could in order to stay healthy in these conditions. That helped a lot.

The results of my parents' hard efforts to prepare us kids and themselves to stay healthy is self-evident and a true testament to their perseverance. None of us ever really felt the chill or caught colds for that matter. My dad would playfully say that I was too slow to catch cold. Case in point, we never saw the doctor once while we were there, and furthermore, I can't recall even passing by the hospital let alone visiting it.

I'm sure everyone can remember to some degree what it's like during this particular phase of life, those formidable get-out-there-and-go-with-gusto years, get-on-out-there-and-experience-everything years. Well, Kodiak Island was turning into a paradise island for us kids, and it just kept getting better and better every day.

After the snow had accumulated over the next few days or perhaps a few weeks, we had enough to roll fist-size snowballs to hurl at each other in a friendly snowball fight. I got my first snowball within a few minutes of stepping out of the house—right upside my head. It didn't hurt at all, but I was stunned, and the cold snowball stuck to the side of my head like the earmuffs I was thankfully wearing at the time. Up to this point there had been many incredible ideas I had to stop being so incredulous of and just accept, like the idea that paper came from wood and glass came from sand, and now I had to accept that this white fluffy stuff called snow was once cold water, raindrops to be more precise, which made no practical sense at all to me. And now they were throwing balls of frozen water called snow at me? Okay, game on!

Snow truly is a great substance for kids with their boundless energy to be playing in it. I absolutely loved the crunchy sound snow made every time I walked across it. If I wasn't busy dodging friendly snowball fights, I was making trails in the snow. Trails that circled back on each other and crossed over each other several times, all in the effort to hear that crunchy sound my boots and snow made together.

Tim and I both got our first snow sleds that first year as Christmas gifts, which translated into a whole different approach to more fun in the snow. Somebody, I think it was gifted to the entire family, also received a nice three-person toboggan from Santa that Christmas. The toboggan was great because it held three of us at one time, which meant three times as much fun sliding down the hill together. We definitely had our fair share of downhill wipeouts, and with those crash-type wipeouts we were experiencing, especially during those first several attempts, could almost be seen as deliberate. In fact, I soon would realize that most, if not all, of those crashes were completely intentional. Was this the only way to stop a toboggan? Crash and tumble off the toboggan just for the fun of it. I get it, sort of like "crash and snow" instead of "crash and burn."

Sledding and tobogganing was a major experience for us kids, and we had such a blast with endless hours of going about playing in the snow as young kids will do.

What a beautiful sight to see all these wonderful snow-covered hillsides in our immediate area, with some of the nearby hills and slopes being well groomed for the locals to use as a community winter wonderland of skiing and sledding had mediocre sloping grades that were perfectly suited for the young novice snow-playing kid like myself. Though a more serious skier might not be so pleased with the skiing conditions on these lazy, rolling hills, I sure was.

For the first several weekends, these well-manicured hillsides were our favorite area to go visit and play in the snow during our weekend outings, which as it turns out, seemed to be the favorite destination for many other people in the community. This was especially obvious on the weekends and gave us a chance to mingle with the community as everyone went about enjoying their time in the snow.

Watching people on skis definitely aroused my competitive nature and only encouraged me to participate more. Skiing looked to be about as much fun as just about anything I'd ever seen. I had no idea how fast those people were going as they skied down those manicured hillsides, but fast enough, and it sure looked like a lot of fun to me.

So far, our coexistence on Kodiak Island was turning out to be the type of adventurous lifestyle most kids would dream about or, in this case, read about … And truth be told, we were living it … and loving every bit of it.

When Dad's Away, the Kids Will Play

My dad was mostly busy where he worked all week long, and sometimes he didn't even come home until the weekend. Now it was because my two older brothers were in school during the weekdays, that I was relegated to play and entertain myself around the yard with Lizzie. Our combined inquisitiveness coupled with my creative imagination kept us occupied for many hours. Entertaining myself all day long came naturally to me, and to be perfectly honest, I was okay with that because I had my real good pal Lizzie to keep me company, and more truth be told, the two of us were quite comfortable playing in the outdoors together, especially when we played in the creeks where we could literally get lost.

It wasn't always about having free-spirited fun all day long. On more-severe winter days we were forced to stay indoors, and in doing so, we tended to develop cabin fever. This affliction can pretty much get the better of anybody, so in order to keep from suffering too much boredom, we found our own little fun distractions to pass the time away.

My mother loved the outdoors as much as us kids, and proved this fact on many different occasions, but she also loved to read books. I was too young to read yet, but I managed quite well to find ways to entertain myself. My mother was always prepared for those types of harsh wintery days, and if she wasn't reading, she was crocheting something. She was quite good at crocheting too. She made many different, useful items of clothing for all of us to wear. She would crochet skullcaps, a.k.a. beanies, as well as always-useful afghan blankets. She would even crochet her own dishcloths for hand washing the dishes.

Dish washing was yet another one of those chores that would soon become a familiar experience for me. I'll say it now: sometimes washing dishes could be just as boring as cabin fever itself could be. As a matter of fact, if I'm not mistaken, it was during one of those more harsher winter storms where we were unable to play outdoors that I was first handed a dishcloth and shown how to wash dishes We kids had both household and outdoor chores, with the outdoor chores being more to my liking that's a fact. Of course I didn't really have outdoor chores yet, so all I did during the outdoor chores was walk around and watch everyone. I mean I tried to help in the little small backyard garden, but come on, lets face it, vegetables at this time were not of my best interest. So for the time being, most house chores were more kid friendly and certainly more controllable for me at this stage of my life. Both of my parents considered these domestic lessons important, and they expected us to learn and execute these chores whenever they deemed it necessary, no questions or excuses.

These winter months were a perfect time for my mother to introduce a few of the house chores to us by means of having fun. Think of it as a testing ground. After a short period given for the learning process, my parents would then cut us loose and supervise us from a distance, always making sure we were doing it right, or nearly right . . . or without disastrous results anyway. Once us kids were getting more proficient at these chores, my dad mostly would from time to time, walk up to me and correct me for possible taking too long without actually getting anything accomplished. It was then, that I was truly entertaining myself. It was all part of the course. I have to admit, I was pretty good at vacuuming but not so good at dusting furniture. I, like many other kids of that age, had the propensity of knocking things over.

Both my parents made it quite clear to us kids that playtime came after the business of house chores. A dirty house was never acceptable. Chores always trumped playtime no matter what. That type of logic makes a lot of sense actually, but not necessarily to the young minded. This was one of those lessons I just couldn't understand at first, as it made no sense at all to me. It was as if my parents couldn't understand what I was telling them. And that was, that if I were allowed to go outside and explore the entire area, that through my many great adventures I could actually discover some hidden buried treasures that nobody else knew about, and if I were just given the appropriate amount time to attempt this then we'd all be rich. All this was just waiting to be discovered … by me.

Being confined in the house on bad weather days certainly could get a kid down, and being given chores to do almost felt like adding insult to injury. But then mom had a way of letting us kids know that nothing could be as bad as we could make it sound. It's important to know that some things in life are necessary and have to be dealt with, no matter what they are or whether or not we want to do them. There were no real actual concerns or worries on my part, though; I just didn't like the idea of work before play.

My first domestic responsibilities were of the commonsense variety. Common sense? What was common sense? There are many examples of what common sense is, and for my first understanding of the word was in the form of realizing that our dog, Lizzie, had to be fed on time and needed fresh water always available while understanding why she depended on us for those things. It was also knowing that the trash always had to be removed from the house so as not to attract mice and had to be put in its own little receptacle outside the house. Those were to be my first chores, and I was not to ever forget them.

Responsibility for an animal's well-being is a very serious matter, and I would soon realize that Lizzie actually relied on me and everyone else in the house for her fresh water, food, and the occasional opening of the front door so she could run, go do her business and get back before the T.V. commercials were over.

Looking back on it now, I think I was given these chores to learn certain lessons as a routine practice, and also because I wasn't quite big enough to do any other serious chores like vacuuming yet. At first attempt, trying to vacuum the carpet was a much bigger challenge for me. After all, this was a 1950s-style cordless sweeper. Oh yeah, I mean I was already quick at offering my assistance with most chores around the house, and for some obscure reason this carpet sweeper held a great fascinating for me. As I previously mentioned, this vacuum cleaner was cordless, which in those days meant no vacuuming power either! Completely operated by man-powered these push-from-behind mechanical cleaners had no electric vacuum pump to suck up the dirt; only raw elbow grease could get these sweepers to work properly—that and the proper height to get a good angle. Alas, I possessed neither at this time of my life, and so I was given a free pass on that job for the time being.

Subtle, yet I Get the Point

It didn't matter if the weather conditions were mild or harsh outside, every day at our home started off with a great breakfast, followed by a great lunch, and ending with a hardy dinner. Education comes to us all through various avenues.

Now, for example, as each day started anew, my mother would go about her usual business of cooking breakfast for everyone as we kids went about our normal business and finished getting dressed for the day. Having a routine and sticking to that routine is normal for everyone, as is learning by observation—OJT, on-the-job training.

And of course daily conversations along with influential and subtle reminders taught us kids the proper way of conducting ourselves with respect to others—the dos and don'ts of life. I'm getting ahead of myself here, but when we took our walks into town, my mother taught us how to stay safe and to keep a watchful eye on the lookout for trouble and danger of all kinds on the trail, as well as in the city or town limits. We kids learned to understand the importance of sticking together while being allowed to roam unrestrained. We were also schooled to understand that we were never allowed to be unruly, bratty, or destructive for no good cause.

Once we reached the outskirts of town, my mother would take a moment to express to us kids that no matter how we were feeling at any given time, we had to behave ourselves, which was as important as watching out for traffic. Watch out for cars and trucks when crossing the streets! Two wise pieces of advice.

Here's a little ditty to remind just about everyone, no matter what age, what to do before crossing any street of any size: "Stop, look, and listen before you cross the street. Use your eyes, use your ears, then you use our feet." My parents constantly presented these and other lessons to us for our own benefit.

In no time at all we kids began to display these same social actions with a subconscious sense of acuity. As far as my mother was concerned, a healthy body included eating the right foods, enjoying the outdoors, and getting physical exercise in any form, i.e. hiking or walking, all the while being mindful of others' rights as well as keeping track of our own. Respect others, and they will respect you. Respect yourself and others will respect you!

WINTER SPORTS

It was about this time in my life when I was beginning to believe I knew just about everything there was to know about having fun in the snow.

Snow, I found out, could be used in many different fun-filled, sports-like ways. I say sports-like because playing in the snow was an actual physical workout, plus we learn how to play with sportsman like conduct. Just having fun playing in the snow all day long was a perfect workout for sure, but engaging in a snowball fight could turn into an all-out neighborhood free-for-all. Seriously though, it didn't take long before I thought I knew all there was to know about how to play outdoors in the snow—from my first time walking across new-fallen snow and hearing that incredibly cool crunching sound the snow made when giving way to my weight, to the pinnacle of mastering the snowy hillsides while sledding at our favorite ski slopes, which we visited practically every weekend during the winter months.

Of course this personal construct lasted only a brief time, and eventually my eyes were opened to a whole new winter sport, when for the first time in my life I saw people skimming across a frozen lake, going faster than anything I'd ever seen before, other than a car or maybe an airplane, that is to say. These people were skating! And skimming faster around that lake than I could fly down any steep hill on my waxed-up sled that's for sure. Faster than some of the birds flying overhead.

I don't believe I had never ever seen this before, and even if maybe I had seen it before on television, there's just no comparison as it just looks so much different in person, seeing it in real time. I watched ice-skating on *Wide World of Sports* sometime later after my first recognition of the activity, but seeing something up close and personal like iceskating feels different somehow, than when watching it on T.V. It looks and feels much different in that it's right there. Of course most TVs in those days were black and white, and screen clarity was compromised even more by extremely poor antenna reception. FYI, back in 1961, a family sitting down together for an afternoon of television viewing might just change the channel to *Wide World of Sports*, which ultimately showcased winter sports. Most of the time our black-and-white television sets displayed a fairly clear picture. However, the problem of "hazy TV screen" usually occurred, with a vengeance I might add, during sports programs. We often struggled to watch the athletes performing their individual skills in the winter white snow. Ahh the performance of the early 1960's black and white television sets.

Contributing to this near-constant dilemma with our early black-and-white television set was poor reception, probably due to the distance from the transmitter itself or obstructions like trees or hillsides. The poor reception caused the television screen to act out on its own with either an intermittent or constant flow of wavy lines running across the screen in various directions, leaving us with an extremely snowy picture screen with distracting wavy lines that would distort the figures and shapes of whatever was on the screen. Honestly, sometimes I had more difficulty trying to make sense of what I saw on television than throwing a snowball accurately. I mean, what in the world? Where was the sanity? That's pretty much how it was for us kids when watching televised sports on a 1960's black and white T.V. set. So just how did I get caught up on ice-skating?

For us, weekends usually were a great time around my house because we usually took a nice drive around the area, looking for a good places to visit and have a picnic. One particular winter day, we went out for a drive and happened upon one of the local frozen lakes. We had gone on several winter outings before this particular time, but never to this lake area. This day started out just like any other outing had before with the car loaded down with everything we could possibly need to have a great picnic. This included carefully loading our toboggan and our sleds and then of course ourselves and Lizzie. Hoping into the little family car and after deciding on which direction to travel, off we'd go. Actually there was much more than simply jumping into the car. But after successful negotiations and efficiently aligning ourselves into our prearranged car seats, we were off, heading out for yet another fun day at any one of our favorite snow-covered playgrounds—so it appeared at first anyway. After several weekends and weekend outings, everyone seemed to be settling in and were getting accustomed to, as well as familiarized to these outdoor picnics in the snow, even having our favorite places to go. As far as we kids knew, this particular weekend excursion was going to be just as much fun as all the previous weekends had been prior. Plus Lizzie always seemed to enjoy the time she had running around in all the fresh snow, spending most of her time pausing and sniffing around, all the while keeping her eyes on all of us.

It was during that time of the year, that all of the lakes in this area were frozen over. Of course after we parked the car, we all got out and walked around for a little while picking up sticks for kindling and larger chunks of dry wood laying on the ground all in an effort to build us a little camp fire for our weenie roast. Us kids helped out too, but mostly played around in the snow. Standing near the edges of the lake, we couldn't help but notice, and eventually stare out across the lake, watching scores of people gliding effortlessly every which way across the smooth icy surface of this huge lake having a lot of fun doing so. All the while I was looking out across the lake, l couldn't help but notice small heaps of snow sporadically piled up throughout the ice-skating area. These random snow heaps were in fact the results of the efforts of many volunteers who had gotten to the lake earlier than the other skaters and spent some serious time behind wide scoop shovels clearing away the loose snow. This was done to make the frozen surface as smooth as possible for unimpeded ice-skating. Of course my perception was these conveniently located piles of snow had been piled up and left there for us kids to play on.

That particular lake must have been the town's favorite lake to skate on, because it looked as if the whole town had showed up to the lake that day.

Now don't misunderstand me; sledding and tobogganing are right up there at the top of being some of the best ways to have fun in the snow. But let's face the facts here: ice-skating looked pretty darn cool too. I mean these ice skaters were flying around on the ice at top speeds! Oh yeah, I couldn't wait to partake in this new sport.

The only key element missing was that I didn't have any skates of my own. No worries though, because that little problem was solved by the very next weekend. I suppose Tim and I must have expressed a greater interest in ice-skating than we thought, because later that week my mom went out and bought the two of us our very own little beginner ice skates, the type designed for children. Basically these were skates with two blades per skate, which made it easier to our balance. Not only did the extra blade support our ankles thus keeping us kids upright as well, but also helped to encourage us kids to stand up straighter using our legs more as we tried to mimic the other skaters. All of whom appeared to need only the single blade. In my case, two blades are better than one. Having two blades on each skate helped me out a lot at first, giving me that extra balance I so very much needed.

My dad and brother Fitzo showed very little interest in this particular sports activity, so it was just my brother Tim, my mom, and me. Actually my mom was pretty knowledgeable about skating and knew just what to do when it came to lacing up our shoes and hitting the ice. She was our coach and gave Tim and me the necessary pointers on how to achieve the proper skating form. As soon as she was through with her coaching advice and getting us all laced-up, Tim and I stepped out onto the edge of the lake and hit the ice for our very first experience of ice-skating … and hit the ice we did, as first-timers will. Literally, our faces went right smack-dab into the snow. w at first we didn't skate, we flopped, or basically we rolled with the snow. It got to the point where I was really starting to appreciate those snow heaps; that's for sure. Maybe that was part of why those small heaps of snow were so conveniently positioned across the lake surface, so people like me could stop for a while. Basically, this ice-skating lesson of ours went on for quite awhile until we finally got the proper hang of skating, or at least until we stopped falling down so much were we could remain vertical on the ice for a longer period of time than at first attempt. Ultimately we achieved the level of success where we'd spent more time on our skates than on our butts int the snow heaps.

Brother Tim and I quickly learned that there was one major downside to having two blades side by side like on our skates: inevitably loose snow would pack tightly up between the blades, and as a result, our skates just wouldn't properly glide the way they were designed to do. For every leg stroke we took, our skates would pack with that much more snow between those twin blades, eventually weighing us down like mud packed shoes. So I wasn't as uncoordinated as first thought since all this time it was this snow that was weighing our little legs down causing us to fall down all the time. This snow buildup prevented us from gliding as skaters are supposed to. In other words, if too much snow built under foot, down we would go. This routine went on for quite some time as we found ourselves sitting on our butts, and scraping the snow out of skates. It looked like Tim and I were constantly forced to take more and more short, breaks for our routine ice-skate clean-out. These random delays weren't discouraging, and before long Tim and I were back out there to try again. Of course after a brief effort of trying to skate around again, bam, our skates would once again have to be cleaned out from all the snow built-up. Like I said, I wasn't too bothered by all of this, because it was my dad who had to clean our skates of all the snow. Like I said, it really was very convenient and extremely nice to have those piles of snow to sit on while we took the time to clean our skates.

It turns out that I was destined to fall whether it was with two blades or one on my skates, I was still going to fall down, kids do. I was like one of those cartoon characters I had always loved to watch on television, the ones that always made me laugh because they were always falling down. What can I say, I was reminded and now I'd become that cartoon character.

As Tim and I were busy taking our lumps and bumps from falling on our butts all morning long, my mother was busy ice-skating like a professional out with the rest of those ice skaters. Turns out, my mother was an accomplished ice skater herself. Who knew? I sure didn't. It was an esoteric sort of revelation for me. My mom was better than pretty good at ice-skating, I mean after she laced up her own ice-skates, she hit the ice like a pro and kept on skating until we could no longer identify her from all the other ice skaters. Oh yeah, she was pretty good at iceskating and it showed right from the very beginning. It sure was great to have someone in the family that was so good at this sport. At least one of the family can represent us here. Watching my mother skate around us gave us more understanding of how to go about properly skating beside the encouragement I got to skate just like that. Standing up on my own two feet.

My natural state of unbalance, which is something every child has to master on his or her own, was not the only issue I had to conquer that day. Already working with wobbly legs to begin with due to my age and then attaching two thin metal blades under each of my shoes certainly created an extra level of difficulty to my balance.

The way to which we approached this was by coming back and practicing doing it all over and over again. Get up, fall down, and repeat. With practice, I overcame these occasional challenges, which were obviously increased in difficulty due to my youthful state of adolescence, but were met with and even stronger adolescent desire to persevere and conquer whereby at the same time I would proved to myself that with persistence I could improve and overcome, which in turn really increased my self-confidence.

All in all, I would have to say that even though most of that day's experience was spent wiping our snow-dotted faces and wet butts, we as a family had a great time together learning to skate. I learned a lot more that day really. I found out that there were good, kindhearted people who showed up to the lake early and spent time cleaning the surface so everyone else could skate on the lake free of fresh snowfall. I am especially grateful to them for leaving those heaps of mounded snow. I also learned that my dad didn't like to skate for one reason or another, but that he was willing to help brother Tim and I get our ice-skating on.

We spent the rest of those first winter months learning how to skate like all those other skaters, upright. Though our skating was more confined along the perimeter of that particular frozen lake. Always switching it up as we continued honing our skills in downhill tobogganing and sledding as well.

Needless to say, throughout all these interactions, we were forming a strong family bond toward each other, mainly I think because my mother was such a patient teacher. My dad was being supportive by not interfering with my mother's teaching, because he didn't know much about ice-skating in the first place, and my mother did. He supported us kids by taking us to the lake and hanging out and helping me clean my skates every time I needed. Which was a lot.

ROAD-SKATING

All that ice-skating sure was fun, and we all ended up taking many more weekend excursions out to that lake that winter to have more fun and to practice our skating technique as well as hitting the slopes with our toboggan. We kept visiting these places up to the point when the ice became too thin and unsafe to skate on account of the changing weather.

During those frequent winter weekend outings, we, or rather I, would learn of a new way to have fun while riding in a car on the snow-laden back roads. It seems there was another way to have fun while driving on the way out to our winter wonderland just by paying close attention to the road conditions and of course how well my dad was driving. As long as there was a decent amount of slush on the roads, we stood a good chance of road-skating, or drifting. The road slush was needed in order to have the best time at road-skating.

It all makes sense, now I understood why my dad had bought this little car in the first place. Maybe that wasn't his original intent, but as it turned out, my dad was pretty smart for getting a little car after all. Our little French-made car was actually perfect for the small family that we were. Yes, a little cramped inside, but whenever we got into trouble with road problems, it was usually a quick fix. This little car was great.

Allow me to help present a visual here. First of all, this little car traversed the immediate roads in the area with relative ease. Second, it got great gas mileage, which was a big plus for my parents, and third, our little island hopper of a car was excellent in tight spaces. We could drive this little car practically anywhere and on any road around the island, and it would fit just about any place we needed to.

For example, this one particular time, when we were out driving around making a family day outing, and as we drove we would constantly be on the lookout for a nice place to have a picnic or even just to pullover and stop so as to have a little playtime in the snow. Frequent stops like these were highly important for Lizzie. We always pulled off the road just a bit with the intention to play around in this new area for a while, allow Lizzie to do her thing and after a brief stop, whereby we would generally leave and go look for an even better place. This particular time was no different. After we all loaded back up into the car, and as we were attempting to leave, the car's rear tires began to spin freely in the snow, and we weren't moving. The car was unable to carry us up out of the slushy snow, which had put us in a slight predicament. The rear tires had no traction, so they just spun freely without any actual forward progress, which is a little disconcerting, especially if it's a new experience.

I had no idea what was going on, as this was the first time I had ever experienced such a scary ordeal. I freaked out! I mean, I was in a place of confusion as well as major concern. We weren't moving and my dad wasn't happy at all. I mean, what was going on here? The thought of us all being stuck out in the hinterlands was too much to take. I fell apart and cried.

I still remember that incident to this very day. I'm not really proud of myself for that moment, but those things happen. Actually we never were in any kind of real danger, but as it was my first experience with this type of road hazard, I expressed my concerns. I happened to choose a sheer panic form of expression, but hey, I wasn't even five years old yet.

After realizing our situation, my dad got out of the car and casually walked to the back of the car, in the meanwhile, my mom had scooted over into the driver's seat as though she was familiar with this predicament, and had experience getting the car unstuck. As my mother steered the car, my dad pushed the little island hopper out of the wet, sloppy slush and once on the harder surface, mom just drove the car to a safer place, making sure we were sitting more completely on the firmer, more-solid road surface. The car had plenty of power, but my dad provided the extra weight and traction that was needed. Teamwork! What I didn't know at the time was that my parents had gone through this sort of thing a number of times before, and so that's why nobody was panicking . . . except me.

The first time I experienced this ordeal I was very young, very scared, and completely confused as to what was happening. And after my initial freak-out was over, with my first experience of getting unstuck being successful, I was steadied and quite ready for the next time.

Truth be told, getting stuck in the snow would eventually become just about as much fun as any of the other winter sports activities that I had been involved in up to that point. We managed to get stuck a few more times that same winter, and each time my dad would grumble and walk to the back of the car, while mom would do her part. This little car was so small and compact. I loved that little car, and at one point I actually had the idea in my head that my dad could pick the whole car up by himself, with us in it. Imagine such hyperbole.

My Fifth Birthday ... Boy, That Means a Lot

By the time the ides of March arrived that year, we were no longer enjoying our winter sports as much as the snow and ice that was once our favorite winter playgrounds, were indeed beginning to melt away. And just like that, our winter playtime and sports lessons were over for that particular winter season. We didn't let the melting of the winter snow discourage us, though, as we continued to venture out to new places to enjoy our weekend outdoor picnics. This was when I first began to realize the endless adventures of the local beaches.

It's important to remember that during this time the interior parts of the island, where most of the snow had accumulated over the winter months, were now becoming wet and messy and were now deemed to be hazardous to play around. Watching all that snow and ice slowly melt and disappear day after day was sad. The once beautiful, clean, soft, white, fluffy element to play in was now unfit to do basically anything but watch it slowly return to it's original rainwater once again and melt away running the creeks down into the ocean.

The upside to all this was that spring was coming, and moreover, since I was born in the springtime, in April to be specific, that also meant my birthday was fast approaching. I would soon be turning five years old, the proper age to start kindergarten. Like most everything else, I could hardly wait to experience this, and what child doesn't like the idea of another birthday? Knowing that my birthday was coming up made the idea of all that snow melting seem less troubling.

April is a great month in itself, and by the time the middle of April arrived, all I was concerning myself with was my upcoming birthday. "Exactly what day is it again?" I would constantly ask. "Exactly what day is my birthday again?" Of course I had to rely on both my parents for several years to remind me what month and day it was for me to celebrate. Patiently they would remind me once again. "Soon" is pretty much all I remember them telling me. My birthday was coming up soon. When I persisted, they would change it up by saying "at the end of the month." I would then ask, "The end of the month? And just when is that exactly?" It was a great display of patience by any child. "Whatever day that is, just keep me informed please, because that's a big day, and we're gonna party. Right?"

Most everybody gets excited about his or her upcoming birthday, and I was most definitely no different. After all, I was turning five years old for crying out loud. I felt different too for some peculiar reason. It was sort of like I was beginning to feel braver. Insecurity, if I ever really experienced it, was certainly no concern of mine by now. A certain sense of boldness and that typical young-boy bravado had now taken a much firmer hold of me.

For instance, eight months earlier when we'd first begun taking our walks into town, I had been a hand-holder. I would voluntarily hold on to my mother's hand, and even liked holding hands. But as time progressed, I began to refrain from holding hands. Eventually, as when we would walk to town, no longer did I hold back. Nope, not me, not this kid, not anymore, not gonna happen. It was all my mother could do to keep Tim and me from running down the hillside trail into town in record time. Even Lizzie seemed to sense the changes. Ever the watchdog, though, Lizzie would never let Tim or me out of her sight—neither would my mother for that matter. I may have felt older, but Lizzie and my mom knew better.

Of course, once we reached the edge of town, we kids would behave in a straighten-up-and-fly-right manner, as our parents had routinely reminded us to do. Yeah, I believe "Straighten up and fly right" was my dad's favorite go-to statement to get us kids to mind him, especially if he thought we were getting unruly or on the verge of getting out of hand. It usually didn't take much for our parents to get our attention either, especially with words like that. My dad used that old attention-getting saying all the time with us kids. My mom would occasionally use it too, but when she used it, we were most likely being too goofy at the time and nothing more, as boys will be boys. Tim and I weren't all that unruly, but I suppose because we were boys we both had that certain propensity to be a bit out of control from time to time and not realize it. Those remarks were only meant to remind us kids that we were getting out of control and needed to scale it back a bit. If we continued with that sort of behavior, we would be punished by some means.

Those remarks worked too. When we heard those words or something similar, we knew to heed what was being said and not to continue with whatever it was that we were doing, or else we would have to face the consequences. Punishment for us meant perhaps not getting to watch TV for a certain period of time or perhaps not being allowed to go outside and play with the neighbor kids for a day or so. The ultimate punishment was not getting desert that evening. Back then we didn't have much of anything as far as in-home entertainment, so for us being grounded was a severe and truly boring form of punishment. Nobody likes getting punished, so it was all about mindful behavior on our part from that first initial warning. Did I happen to mention that my dad was a retired chief petty officer for the US Navy? I believe he held on to some military perspectives.

Now because I was getting older and about to turn five, my parents were expecting me to be more responsible for my actions. They told me so on many occasions. Remember those ice skates? They didn't come without a price after all. The price I paid for those skates was a much different form of payment than what my parents paid. That's right; with a gift like that, my parents expected me to reciprocate by paying attention to them and doing what I was told to do. After all, they had my best interests at heart. Deep down inside I think I knew that.

All those seemingly endless adages, guidelines, and instructions that my parents were so intent on us kids knowing weren't for their enjoyment but rather for our betterment. They were a type of assurance for an easier, more understanding, and content life. It was advice that would stand the test of time. And getting along with others meant just that. They were trying to teach us kids how to live properly and how to get along in society while at the same time not being naive to the world affairs going on around us. Eventually this would all make perfect sense to me. But I wasn't at that age yet, and at the age of five, kids still need to be reminded and advised of those important and necessary lessons of life. Sometimes those lessons were strictly enforced in order to emphasize their importance.

I'm very grateful to have been taught these lessons at such an early age rather than having to realize them for myself later in life. Everyone should be grateful for the lessons they learn, especially the free lessons.

Frozen Crab Leg Anyone?

It's pretty plain to see that living on Kodiak Island sure had its benefits in many ways, and one of the more recognized is that of daily, fresh-caught seafood. Living in such close proximity to the ocean waters ensured us of that.

We kids were learned everything about how to live among our new neighbors and about their different culture, which was obviously quite different from the culture of our previous home in California; that's for sure. One of these big cultural differences was, as I just pointed out, the convenience of locally caught seafood. Indeed, living on that wonderful island paradise sure had its perks.

One of my most cherished memories from that time of my life would be us kids snacking on frozen crab legs. My mother approved of everybody eating good snack foods and had explicitly impressed upon us kids to do just that, and frozen crab legs qualified as a healthy snack. It was common understanding by now just how important it was to eat good, healthy meals throughout the day. Starting with a good breakfast, maintaining good eating habits throughout the day, and finishing with a good, hearty meal for dinner was the cornerstone to any healthy lifestyle, and everything we snacked on in between meals was important. Believe me, eating healthy snack foods was just as enjoyable for us as any other type of snacks. Actually, we never knew any other type of snacks were available, so it was as easy for us to eat frozen crab legs as anything else. Basically, we gave it no never mind probably thinking this is what everybody snacked on. Naïveté in its finest and purest form.

Fresh or frozen, crab legs were at the top of everyone's list. If any of us kids were outside playing and got hungry, all we had to do was go open up the chest freezer in the one-car garage attached to our house, reach in, dig around for the right size piece, and grab a single frozen king-crab leg. This chest freezer stood too tall for me to actually reach in by myself, so I always had to either drag a stool over to climb up on, or simply ask Tim to help me fish out a piece of crab. The crab legs always thawed out rather fast, so our crab-sicles didn't stay entirely frozen for long. I don't know what made those crab-sicles so tasty good. Something special about eating frozen crab legs that had us kids going back for more, time and again. Neither mom nor dad ever served us frozen crab for dinner, it was always heated up. But there us kids were, enjoying frozen crab-sicle legs on any given day while living on Kodiak Island.

Walking down to the harbor every day to buy fresh-caught seafood was no harder than picking up our mail at the local post office. We just walked on down and inquired from a local fisherman. There had to be at least ten different fishermen willing to sell part of their day's catch. After all, that was exactly how they made a living. That easy.

My dad seemed to favor buying in larger quantities, so that was why my folks bought a chest freezer. That way we always had something or another in large quantities waiting for us in the freezer.

With king crabs being so abundant in the waters off the coast of our immediate area, it appeared that we would never be without any crab legs to eat. However, we also had our other favorite types of seafood in the freezer, like local halibut, salmon, and gulf shrimp.

MAKING FRIENDS

By the spring of 1961, my family had been living on this beautiful island sharing in its many wonders for better than half a year. And even though not one person in my family said anything out loud to anyone else, I'm inclined to believe that there was an all-around consensus regarding our contentment on this island. I believe every single one of us was quite happy and content living on Kodiak Island to the point of not needing to say anything. It truly was just about the best place in the world for any kid to be. To me it just had to be.

There were so many really cool places to go and things to do year round with fascinating lifestyle changes. Even with all this fun to be had, my parents still weren't finished teaching us kids the variables of life. Apparently, by taking us kids to all these different locations and getting us involved in outdoor sports that involved other people, my parents were in fact teaching us how to properly interact with others while familiarizing ourselves with our surroundings, all in the guise of having fun together. Now, of course hanging out together as we did is the natural way families interact, which is good. Bonding and familiarizing yourselves with each other is one of the healthiest things to do with your family by far.

Even though we kids had gotten to know quite a few of the local people in the immediate area and had developed an even larger perspective of the immediate area, my parents encouraged us to get more involved, and with some of the community activities. It was another great way of meeting other people in the community so I was up for it. Involving ourselves with the community meant that we were going to participate in activities with other kids from the surrounding area that were around our own age. Apparently, my parents were rather keen on the idea of us kids getting involved. They often reminded us that the word *participate* also means "share." So we kids learned to share our time with others, which is to say we learned to participate with others in various activities.

Everyone in my family had friends in his or her own age group by now, but just being friendly wasn't enough. Having fun with a few friends and staying comfortable with just that would be encouraging our own limitations. It's important to do many fun things with friends, all the while learning that particular important lesson of making new friends. I always seemed to make new friends wherever I traversed but that might be because I was looking for friends. Some people were not as easy to make friends with as others, but that didn't mean they were unapproachable. I learned a great deal from this, including that to participate with others really is to share what we know. Both words relate to each other, like a hand in glove.

So just what were we going to be doing with these other kids? You never can tell what children are capable of imagining. For me, I had heard of activities like swimming and fishing and kayaking. Of course I was no novice when it came to exploring either. And since I could ice-skate pretty well, I figured I would be okay with these other new activities. Community activities like sports or church (or a faith congregation of an individual's choice) or any other appropriate activity that involves kids around the same age is always a good idea. Kids should participate in something positively constructive that can create a certain amount of healthy personal pride—pretty much anything that gets kids busy outdoors with other people who want to build a strong community through friendship and bonding.

Fitzo decided to join the local Cub Scout pack as a Bobcat, and Mom would eventually become the Den Mother, which meant that some of those Cub Scouts would be coming over to our house for their weekly meetings. I have no fond memories Fitzo' cub scout meetings, as overtime those kids came over to the house for there cub scout meeting,

I would be ushered out of the room and told to stay in the other rooms away from the group of scouts. It's possible that maybe I was told to stay in the other rooms while the other kids were over for more-serious matters because I was after all, a very loquacious young boy.

Being involved in activities with other people in the community helps a person recognize his or her own potential and become more comfortable with the differences in us all. Not only did I learn that many people tend to have unusual customs—which were certainly different from what I was used to—but I also learned that there are differences in all people, and that's why it's so very important to accept these differences and learn from them as well.

Now since my brother Tim and I were too young for the Cub Scouts at the time, the two of us ended up joining the local Sunday-school youth activities group. Kids our age and a little older were meeting at the local church and spending the afternoon together doing all sorts of fun stuff. It was my parents' idea, and so far in my very young life they had impelled me into a world of adventure and fun, so why should I not trust them now?

The first day of Sunday school was a very exciting moment for me. I mean it was the typical first time, meet and greet that everyone experiences, and it pretty much plays out the same at any age. Now even though I was a rather gregarious child, I too was a bit apprehensive of meeting all of these new people at first. Those first moments of meeting new people can be pretty awkward at first, then before long everything is getting comfortable and back to normal, where suddenly all the people are having a really great time engaged in friendly conversations.

Another big moment that stands out in my mind from our first day of Sunday school was when the youth pastor came over and presented Tim and me each with our own Bibles before we left. He told us that we could keep these Bibles for our very own and that one day we would read this book for ourselves. These special books were unread and brand new, and the bindings were dark brick red. The youth pastor told us that as soon as we learned how to read, the color of our Bibles would help to remind us that these books were to be read. The youth pastor also told us to remember that the word *Bible* when translated means *book*.

Kodiak Crab Festival

With my fifth birthday celebration a recent memory, my young thoughts, as well as eyes and ears, next focused on the scuttlebutt about the upcoming town festival that we had been hearing so much about for the past several weeks. This unique celebration was all the talk—that and some guy called an astronaut who was soon to be traveling into outer space. I didn't posses the mindset to pay close attention to the general news regarding the astronaut because the idea of it was way over my head at the time. Not to put a pun to it. I'm not sure now if I had ever watch a science fiction movie to that point to form an opinion of whether or not I liked astronauts, let alone try to emulate them. Honestly, at this time, I was more excited about this big town party I'd been hearing so much more about.

The townspeople of Kodiak Island celebrate federal and state holidays just as enthusiastically as any people in the world celebrate any of their own important holidays. And just like everywhere else, the town has its own customary local festivals and celebrations. Kodiak has one particular celebration that is exclusive and unique only to this quaint little island village. The three-day celebration is know as the Kodiak Crab Festival, and as everyone knows, if there's food, the people will come. Put an exclamation point on the festival by offering up fresh cooked crab, and they'll surely not neglect to invite others to come along as well.

Each and every year in May, the entire lower section of the town, including the town's smaller boat harbor, is transformed into a big party location for three fun-filled days celebrating the bountiful king-crab catch from local ocean waters. This celebration also includes the ever so important outcome of bringing people together whereby meeting new people and enjoying each other's company, all the while chowing down on freshly caught, freshly steamed local king crab. People from all over the world have come to this festival to join in and help celebrate with the local Kodiak townspeople.

Of course there is more than just steamed crab being offered to the festival crowd to enjoy. Indeed, as with any other festival, one day an area is all calm and quite as usual, and the very next day it's bustling with all sorts of different booths and cordoned-off areas readied for the opening-day ceremonies.

As my family and I strolled the grounds of this venue, I was introduced to the idea that these festival booths were independently operated by merchants or vendors selling things from different varieties of foods to beautifully handcrafted jewelry to magnificent handcrafted clothing designed and created by local artisans. Many of these booths offered the same types of sculptured pieces, only sculpted by different artisans from perhaps another area of the island or even another area all together.

There were many various designs of wood-crafted, hand-sculpted figures of eagles, whales, walruses, and the like, all of which were made to honor and resect for all of the local wildlife. But the biggest and baddest-looking of all the carvings, no matter who the artist was that sculpted it, were the sculptures of the mighty Kodiak brown bear. From the very large, almost life size wood-crafted replica to the smallest hand size figurines, the Kodiak brown bear was the most admired of all the wood carvings. Of course that's my personal perspective. Those particular carving pieces automatically caught everyone's eyes. It dominated the attention and interest over all of the other artwork—at least for me it did. Yes indeed, a big Kodiak Island party. Very cool!

Some of the items being sold at this festival are now illegal to be sold in the U.S., though it's important to remember that restrictions had not been put into place by the time restricting people to the sales of certain precious commerce. For example, in those days it was not uncommon for ivory or whale bone to be sold at markets including festivals like the Kodiak Crab Festival of 1961. In fact, in those days, it was completely legal to purchase ivory from any vendor or other individual artisan without particular notice. There were beautifully scrimshawed ivory pieces, crafted by people who certainly had the skill and love for the art world. Their beautiful artistry—etched mainly from walrus tusks, whale bone, and other marine wildlife—was legal for anyone to purchase in those days. Not so nowadays.

Addendum: the indigenous peoples of these Alaskan lands, who are represented by several different respectable and proud groups, are exempt from this Federal law and are allowed to continue to collect and work with these ivory materials, as it has been part of their culture for thousands of years. Ivory tusks may have been outlawed for mainstream usage, and for very good reason, but they remain an important and integral part of the indigenous people's heritage.

By all means, there were many other attractions to be enjoyed at this festival, such as the designated areas set up for the various musicians and the various dancing troupes to perform. But the main theme was king crab, and quite frankly, we were there for the food. Food, glorious food … deliciously prepared food, such as hot venison dinners or maybe just a simple, freshly made caribou burger or maybe even a bear burger.

The vendors that offered their prepared comestibles to the hungry festival spectators weren't just local people, but rather vendors from various areas and ports from around the area. They were all technically chefs, offering various foods of interest—elk, moose, and perhaps red deer, just to name a few—all being served up to the hungry and festive crowd. I even suppose there could have been other freshly caught seafood offered at the festival that day; however, the main food attraction as far as I was concerned was the king crab, and that's what I wanted. Freshly steamed crab. And not just any crab, but king crab. Mounds of hot, steaming king crab with lots of melted butter and a nice thick slice of freshly made sourdough bread to help soak up the excess butter off the plate. Yum-yum.

Along with all of this really great food and beautiful local artwork, there was also singing and dancing being preformed by various ethnic groups. Various dance troupes, from various areas doing dance routines that were both fascinating as well as colorful. No surprise here either, since this was a small fishing village with a diverse ethnic community.

What a great joy it is to have the pictures we took of the 1961 Kodiak Crab Festival. Now I can look at those pictures and be reminded of a beautiful memory, and I can share them with others who were for one reason or another unable to attend. Having these pictures of past events whereby I had participated in, certainly helps me to better remember the parts of my past that I can still recall with reasonable clarity while also helping to refresh my memory of events that I might have otherwise forgotten.

Take for instance the picture I have of a little Alutiiq boy posing with Tim and me at the Kodiak Crab Festival of 1961. At one time or another, we all noticed this little nine- or ten-year-old boy walking around the festival proudly holding on to this large king crab. We weren't the only people to take notice and certainly not the only ones to ask him to have his picture taken with us. It seemed everybody wanted to have a picture taken with him. Maybe it was just because of the way he was holding on tightly to that large creature of the deep, or maybe it was because he was holding on to it as if the world itself would be in deep trouble if he were to let go. I don't remember; I just remember posing next to him and that wickedly huge creature of the sea. There is little doubt in my mind that we kids certainly approached him and his crab with caution. It wasn't him that gave us cause for apprehension but the large crab he was holding on to that gave us this overwhelmingly incredulous feeling of who had a hold of whom. I mean, was that crab still alive or what? That crab he was holding was very very big! As we approached this young Alutiiq boy, we instantly recognized the signature big Native Alaskan smile that is so typical of these strong and noble people. The Alutiiq people are some of the best smiling people in the world and as quick as this young boy was with his smile, he obliged us with a picture of a lifetime. Oh, and by the way, it turned out that the king crab was his own catch.

Supposition can have its rewards, and though nobody really remembers the full story—maybe we never asked him—we all suspected that the little Native boy was there at the festival in order to sell his catch to someone looking to take home some of the day's festivities. I don't know if he ever sold that huge crab, but one thing is for sure: he could have made a bundle of cash that day had he charged just ten cents—big money in those days—for every one of those pictures he took that day. Everyone at that festival wanted to take a picture with him as he held on tight to that huge monster.

Unfortunately, time has sequestered any memory I may have had of interacting or conversing with this little boy, but at least I still have a photo of us posing for this moment in time.

It would be an understatement to say that I immensely enjoyed everything about the festival gathering. That was just the beginning too.

BLANKET TOSSING

Saving the best part for last is not an unusual or uncommon act, and I've saved the best story and most exciting part of this festival for last.

As far as I'm concerned, the most fun thing to do at this festival was to get tossed. I realize that last statement is a little cryptic, but to me, that was all it really was … getting tossed high up into the air by means of a very large blanket.

The Kodiak Crab Festival really was a fun time for all. And based on information from the Internet, they're still having a great time every year—no signs of slowing down or losing interest at all.

Who's ready to go flying again?

Blanket tossing was a common practice for the indigenous peoples, and therefore it was easily adopted by the new settlers and introduced as a fun-filled festival event. Nobody needed a ticket in order to take a turn when it came to the blanket tossing. You just stepped up to the blanket and got tossed.

Now most little kids are extremely comfortable with blankets to begin with. Tie a small blanket loosely around a kid's neck, fashioning it to fly in the wind as the kid runs around, and let the imagination soar. The offer of a good time being tossed into the air is certainly a no-brainer for most people of almost all ages. I think some adults are still very hip to this idea, being young at heart. Therefore, it's easy to see my immediate attraction to this oversize blanket.

We had been standing there, my family and I, along with the other spectators and marveling at how this enormous blanket could toss someone, so high into the air. Blanket tossing may not have been a new concept to these islanders, but it sure was to me. Watching someone being tossed way high up into the air like that was so exciting to me. It looked like the next best thing since flying in an actual airplane.

Blanket tossing involves trusting several people who encircle and grasp the edge of a very large blanket. The person to be tossed stands in the middle of the blanket. Then the trustworthy people holding the outer edges snap the blanket with a quick upward motion, raising the edges up to their chests, and the person in the middle is catapulted high into the air. When that person comes back down, as gravity dictates, he or she softly lands somewhere near the middle of the blanket, with the goal being to stay standing up. The trustworthy blanket brigade continues to tightly hold on to the blanket until that person has landed safely back on the blanket. Then someone gives the signal, and back up into the air the person goes again. This action can go on for several more tosses.

Many of the festival crowd were taking turns being tossed, and eventually, I got my chance at it too. Some people turned down their opportunity to get tossed, but when they asked me, well, I jumped at the chance of course. I was still very light, so the blanket brigade had to adjust to balance out their strength so as to not toss me into nearby tree tops, and though they were a lot gentler with me, I was still able to get some substantial air. As I was tossed high into the air, I felt as if I were flying like a bird. Volant!

Great fun at any age.

GYM? ANYBODY AROUND HERE KNOW GYM?

That blanket-tossing activity at the Kodiak Crab Festival was certainly a fun game for everyone to enjoy, but for the indigenous people of this region it's more than a fun game. Oh, absolutely they have fun at it, but it's also one of the more important ways these people stay in such excellent condition.

It goes without saying that these phenomenally resilient Alutiiq people, as well as the other main tribal people of Alaska, are in tip-top condition. These indigenous people—the Inupiaq, the Yup'ik/Cup'ik, the St. Lawrence Island Yupik, the Aleut, the Athabaskan, the Eyak, the Tlingit, the Haida, and the Tsimshian—also always seem to have a ready smile. It's as if these people go about life's hardships with beautiful readied smiles planted firmly on their faces—every one of them. It's because they're very happy people, and quite content with what they have.

There is definitely more to the game of blanket tossing for these people than merely enjoying the momentary sensation of independent flight. The legacy of this particular activity and many other indigenous sports-like endeavors date to long ago and are actually viewed as a form of physical fitness. The northern tribal people used to rely on other materials for blanket tossing, as they had no cotton in order to make woven blankets like the ones used at the Kodiak Crab Festival. The materials the indigenous people used came from what they had all around them, like properly cured whale skins. They taught themselves how to maintain balance through this act of physical fitness by using a cured whale skin.

Even though blanket tossing was seen as a physical workout, I'll bet it was just as much fun for them as it was for me. These very healthy people realized long ago just how important it was for everyone, especially the ice hunters, to stay in shape at all times in order to return safely to their respective lodges.

In suburbia people go to local fitness centers with the intent of getting themselves into top physical condition and staying that way. Other cultures have the same intent and have their own physical fitness centers of sorts, often with a long history behind the physical activity too.

Many different tribes in the this region practice the art of tossing people into the air in order to hone their balance, a skill so well practiced as to become second nature to each and every hunter. Practically every tribal member will practice this skill so that everyone will develop the ability to navigate safely through the often rough, unstable terrain while successfully negotiating the unstable ice floes.

Balance is truly important in many aspects of life. Try to imagine being a hunter in this area, and think about how important it is to have good balance. Hunting for food along the banks of a frozen river or traversing on ice sheets alongside the frigid water of the Bering Sea, for instance, can be highly dangerous, and if not careful or skilled, it could prove to be a mortal act if ill-prepared. If a hunter, or an unsuspecting day hiker is unprepared and falls, his or her demise is imminent. Alaska is not a good place to be ill prepared, especially if the end result could be a dunk into the freezing waters of the north. Yes indeed! In fact, give it a long thought; mull that thought for a while, and consider that this ordeal is something that hunters must go through over and over again in order to get food for their families. It's easy to understand the valuable teachings of this balance lesson and how it works to everyone's advantage.

A potlatch is a celebratory feast of the Pacific Northwest tribal people. People gather together for friendly conversation and also engage in some sportsmanlike competition that displays individuals' skills. These activities help everyone stay strong and fit while having a good time and connecting with each other. This type of community bonding is very important for any society and is commonly recognized among people all around the world. These strong Alaskan people have been around for ten thousand–plus years, and community gatherings are still key to their societies.

A quick analysis and staunch reminder here: Blanket tossing simulates unstable conditions, like icy shorelines, that tribal members may have to negotiate while out hunting for food or scouting. It takes great balance and upper-body strength to keep from falling backward into the blanket, or icy-cold waters.

While the indigenous people used whale skins, the festival organizers of the Kodiak Crab Festival fashioned a pretty decent substitute using a large, specially designed, heavy-duty blanket for the reenactment. Now the object of this activity is for the person being tossed to land on the blanket as close to the center as possible while remaining standing, without falling or losing total balance. With each following throw, the person on the blanket is elevated higher and higher, while each time coming down as near the center as possible. Some of the participants get as high as twenty feet into the air. The winner of the event is the one who can be tossed the highest while landing on their feet as close to the center of the blanket, or whale skin as possible without losing balance.

The people holding the blanket never tossed me very high into the air, nor did they ever toss me up more than a couple of times. Personally that was a real bummer for me because I actually felt that I was ready for more serious elevation time, when it came to that type of fun. Naturally, the very young always believe they are ready for more. There was no doubt in my mind that I wanted to be tossed up into the air a lot more than those few times, but I now believe that those kind and wise people were more afraid that I might start tossing a little something up of my own if they kept going. They were probably right, and knew from past experiences just how many times a youngster could take being tossed before it was too late. So therefore, without argument from my end, I was timely limited to just a few rounds of "blanket tossing free falling."

Special note: Fishing the extremely cold waters in and around the northern hemisphere is extremely dangerous for anyone, whether the person is completely inexperienced or reasonably well informed. All fishing vessels and their crew members are at risk of mortal danger, whether they be small kayaks or umiaks or much larger commercial-size fishing boats. Extremely dangerous working conditions! Everyone needs to be aware and willing to work on their balance. So start working on your balance everyone.

It's been my experience that all workforces throughout the world face their own difficulties, and that is why we all need to stay patient with others and work to understand them as they gain their balance. Remember, it's very important not to go overboard with things in life, and highly important to maintain an even balance.

THE OUTDOORS WERE
MEANT FOR DISCOVERY

As time marched on, so too continued my daily observational, educational lessons. Just watching how people interacted was a lesson in itself for anyone to take notice, and I did. Since I was a loquacious and gregarious child by nature, I always seemed to be around people as though being drawn to them, and therefore it was natural that I picked up on what they were all doing.

Along with these many lesson I would soon be learning was to obey the laws of the land and of nature with the understanding as to why that was so important for both natures well being as well as for my own well being. At this point in my life, this very important lesson was about respecting the wild, one more lesson to add to the many things I'd previously learned regarding the respect towards nature. This included keeping our hiking trail clean from trash and other man-made articles. This is not to suggest that these public trails, or any other place on the island for that matter, were littered. However, accidents can happen, and wild animals don't pick up litter, consequently it was a lesson for the ages.

My mother was a country girl all the way, and she had every intention to keep the countryside clean by any means. She would explain to us kids that it was about being prepared and realizing that accidents can happen to anyone, and just pitch in and help clean it up. Even if we were the first ones pick up the litter. It was something she'd taken to heart and wanted us kids to absorb and fully understand that no matter whose at fault, it won"t get pickup on pointing fingers or blaming others. The idea is if somebody accidentally or purposely leaves a mess alongside the hiking trail, it still has to be properly taken care of or else it will be there for perhaps the next time we hike our trail. Deal with it! Clean it up even if somebody else is at fault. Garbage looks bad and can make most everyone who sees it uncomfortable. And as I said, animals know no better.

Nearly every weekday during the more favorable months of the year, we would walk that quarter mile down our favorite trail and into town, taking care of what ever business errands my mother may have needed to take care of, which always included going to the Kodiak post office. Our general route into town, down the quarter mile hiking trail, and a quick romp in town typically took us an hour or so before ultimately trekking back up the same trail towards our home. Occasionally, we would choose to walk a different route back home, taking us perhaps more travel time to get back home, while indeed other times this short favorite hiking trail of ours would itself become our perfectly good reason for an extended hike as we meandered the trail picking the many various ripe berries that were in season seemingly at the time and all season long.

During our daily excursions into town we would encounter wildflowers and berry bushes seemingly everywhere. I understood and recognized those bushes almost from the very first time I saw them. And for good reason too; because when those various berries were in season and ripe to perfection, we couldn't help but pause our hike in order to eat up as many of the sweet wild berries as we could. We always ate to our complete and satisfactory content, stopping ourselves just in time before experiencing the dreaded berry-belly bloat. There were wild strawberries, salmonberries, and other berries I had a hard time pronouncing. A very berry island indeed.

I eventually started recognizing many of the different types of wildflowers on my own as well. In fact, I learned rather quickly that not all of the islands wildflowers were as nice to smell as some of the others. Some of them being very pretty to look at, perhaps maybe even to touch, but the sense of smell was not rewarded by some. Flowers seem to attract children in a magical way like flowers attract honey bees. I remember my attraction to these beautiful flowers included some of the funny names that were given to them. Names like snapdragon, orchid, and, my favorite, monkey flower, or yellow mimulus.

The island's berry bushes and wildflowers grew just about everywhere and was truly an awe inspiring sight to see growing along the hillside trail amongst beautiful evergreen trees.

BURIED TREASURE

Besides my own personal experiences of life, I was also learning through others' experiences and how they handled themselves in unexpected situations. I mean, I wasn't the kid who found the treasure, but I was there when it was discovered. Let's see here …

This one particular summer day as we were preparing to go for our daily hike into town, Fitzo had decided that he would join us on our trek. I should have known something different was about to happen, as he usually didn't walk into town with us, so this was an event already in the making.

We had just finished with the drop-offs and pickups at the local post office, the last of our daily routine stops, and had started our hike back up the trail toward home when it all started to really get different. Fitzo, in typical form, was not really with us, as he walked ahead of the rest of us up the trail by quite a ways. Suddenly he left the main trail and began fooling around in the taller grass a little ways off the main trail. This only encouraged my brother Tim and I as soon as we heard and saw him rummaging around in the tall grass like that. It's instinctual for kids to realize when treasure is about to be discovered, so we too got more than curious and took off running to see what he had found. Our mother asked him, Tim asked him, even I gave it a shot and asked him what he found. But neither time did he respond, which only intrigued us further.

Jumping at the chance to see in no time at all we had gathered by the edge of the trail ready to lend support, and a helping hand to in what he had found. Lizzie was as captivated by all this commotion as the rest of us were, and she intently investigated the excitement for herself, heading to Fitzo's exact location. Once there she added her own equal enthusiastic encouragement to his discovery but making it look like she was digging too. Still he remained mum as to what he'd found, while leaving us all clueless, and quick to hypothesize. He remained defiantly silent to everyone's questions as he continued to be equally mysterious. Being secretive was Fitzo's typical approach to everything; it was just the way he was. We were just gonna have to patient and wait to see what he had found.

And just what did he find? How did he even know to look in that area of grass in the first place? *Is this how buried treasures are found?* I wondered. *Aw, come on, I'm young, and I want to know.* His continued silence only added to our already heightened expectations, to the point that I was beginning to grow impatient. We didn't really know what to expect, so by this time I was imagining all sorts of possibilities.

As Tim and I stood on the trail alongside my mother, she took this opportunity to tell a story about gold. Even thought we had already heard these particulars before, it was still a very interesting and exciting story for me to hear again. A story of how shiny gold had been discovered all over Alaska. Shiny Gold! Yup, sounded nice already! Okay, maybe she never exactly said "shiny gold," and used more phlegmy in her description of gold, just as she probably took that particular moment to remind us that our dad and his friend Mr. G. Cornelius had invested in a small land claim of their own. From the way the story went, It sounded to me like my dad and his friend staked out some land, and then proceeded to go about digging around on this piece of land, looking for rocks. Had I known this earlier, I could have offered my services, as I looked for rocks all the time in our backyard. Afterwards I had heard that It was also no secret they never found any gold. Not on that particular piece of real estate anyway, but they shared in big dreams. Yeah, come to think of it, I had heard that story once before.

Mom just forgot she had already told us. Tim and Fitzo had probably heard that story a few times by then.

Reminding us kids of the possibility of gold being discovered in this area only served to intensify how excited I was already getting. Just knowing that something, anything, was about to be pulled up out of the ground, with the potential of a treasure-chest was way more than I could take. Wait a minute, who said anything about it being a treasure-chest. How did it become a treasure chest all of a sudden? And the fact that I was going to bear witness to it was all I could stand. What is it, tell me damn it . . . oops.

We were only too anxious by now to see what all of his digging around had discovered, and as Fitzo slowly made his way back to the trail, I could hear him mutter some words, but couldn't really understand what he was saying, which sounded a lot like giddy, twaddle-type utterances. All I could make out was something that sounded like *madu-bla-bla*. Truthfully, I have no recollection of what he was saying to us as he walked out, after all, I had aimed all of my focus towards that wooden box he was carrying tightly next to his chest.

As he made his way back to the trail with his treasure box, I caught a quick, slightly out-of-focus glimpse of his discovery. It wasn't that large as I had imagined, but he had something in his otherwise diligent hands. He stepped back onto the trail, his face nearly as dirty as his clothes, which only took second place to the little dirt-crusted, decomposing wooden box he had just lifted out of the ground. I guess it goes to show that most kids have a hard time staying clean no matter how small the task. Based on his appearance, I would have guessed that he had actually found a much larger treasure, and the box he was holding onto actually held the giant key it was gonna take. But who was really paying attention to size anyway? Treasure is treasure, right? I just wanted to know what was inside the box. Was it gold? What did gold even look like anyway? It just had to be gold. At last he spoke his first discernible words: "It's a box."

Well duh, wait what? Well that's great news, but we already knew that! I thought. Just a short time earlier I had been imagining all sorts of great possibilities, and now he'd announced that it was just a half-buried wooden box with no significant connection to gold mining whatsoever? But wait, technically it was still buried treasure. Right? It just didn't happen to be the size and shape I was imagining at first.

Fitzo fastidiously scraped more of the crusty dirt off around the edges of this treasure chest, as though he had all the time in the world. Crazy man. Did he not know of any quicker way to open the box? Of course no is the answer to that rhetorical question as he continued his method. It took a little while longer for him to scrape off practically every bit of the remaining dirt in my view, in order to find the seams and ultimately the latch to this old box. I think we all realized that day that I was far too young and impatient when it came to treasure hunting. *Open this damn thing up already!* I thought. Yes, kids swear too.

In the meantime, I must have calculated multiple theories about what kind of treasure was inside the box, and I was certainly in no condition to wait any too much longer for him to reveal the contents. How much gold could this small, crusty, antiquated box hold anyway? With all of my anxiousness regarding the contents of this small treasure chest, it just couldn't get opened fast enough for me.

There was no key needed after all. When Fitzo finally opened up the box all he had to do was pry the lid off to display its treasures. At first I was momentarily blinded by a bright sunbeam reflecting off the many little sparkly spheres of clear and colored glass. Wait. Is gold shiny or not? Was this gold? What was this? Just a minute, someone say round, shiny glass? No gold!?

Instead of gold, all of us were looking at a box full of small glass spheres of varying sizes—glass marbles. How about that! And though I had never seen gold before, I just knew this wasn't it, because nobody shouted "Gold!" or "Eureka!" Instead, it was, "Oh, how about that, marbles." At least someone knew what this treasure was.

The marbles were pretty to look at and just as exciting to me as actual gold, but then, this wasn't my treasure. Even though no great financial wealth or even one speck of gold was found in this whole exciting ordeal, it was still a really cool discovery. I liked it.

And what about the wooden box? Where did it come from in the first place? Was it a time capsule someone had buried for future kids to find? My mother suggested that someone must have set the box down on the ground several months or even years earlier and forgotten where they had put it. She hypothesized that this activity may have originally taken place higher up the hillside. Then the box may have eventually slid on down the hill. Over time, perhaps during a series of storms, the box could have become mostly obscured from view, with just a small portion sticking out of the ground. Just waiting for someone like Fitzo to spot and dig up.

I remember there being so many exciting things going on all the time back then. Every day was a new adventure for me. I didn't realize at the time just how blessed I was for this type of living.

Because I was having such a great time, I had entirely forgotten all about what it had been like to live in Sunnyvale. I no longer thought of racing to the back door of the house in order to see the trains roll by. I was acclimating to the island all right and by every means available. Some days were more eventful than other days, but every day was momentous to me. New daily events were playing out right before my eyes, and I was taking part in every bit of them.

Imagine that treasure.

How Tall Is That Totem?

Most people see their first totem poles in books and magazines, but some, like my family and I, are fortunate enough to see their first totem pole up close and personal.

My family must have driven past this one particular totem pole at least a hundred times before we decided it was time to walk over and get a good, close-up view. This particular totem pole stood about twenty-five feet and was painted from top to bottom with many bright colors.

Throughout history totem poles have been used to symbolize and represent various tribes and their people. Without a doubt, the indigenous people of Alaska are among the best totem-pole builders. Totems are works of art crafted from logs of certain trees, and specially selected by a highly respected elder of the local tribe.

The totem-building process starts with a group of highly respected tribal members selecting one member to choose a specific tree of a certain size and diameter. There's a lot more to the tree selection than merely picking one out of the forest because the chosen tribal member is most likely a member of high importance and is simultaneously performing an important ritual while selecting the tree.

After the tree has been selected and cut down to its desired length, the master wood-carver of the tribe designs and carves out the different animals that best represent that particular tribe. A totem is like a colorful, descriptive address telling visitors just whose lodge they are walking or floating up to. Not every tribe uses color paints on their totems, but every tribe will stick to a certain pattern and combination of local animals that best represents their area and tribe. The combinations of local creatures can include animals such as local eagles, hawks, crows, cormorants, various fish, seals, otters, walruses, killer whales, mighty king crabs, and the even mightier Kodiak brown bears.

Now after the wood carving is completed, the totem may be painted. Obviously, many different combinations of bright and dark colors are needed in order for the totem to look just right. Once the painting is completed, the totem pole is erected, standing upright.

Various totems stand tall and majestic for all to see, including visitors from great distances—very colorful addresses for all to recognize.

THE FIRST BOY ASTRONAUT
TO LAND ON THE MOON

The first astronaut to land and walk on the moon was a boy? Well, not exactly, not in the actual sense … but sort of.

First off, let me just say that everyone, sometime or another in his or her life, will read or hear about the 1969 moon landing when, with the combined intelligence of scientists in the space program, we succeeded in flying to the moon and back. We're talking about the earth's moon here, and "we" are the citizens of the United States, as well as outside interests, financed this major exploration whereby not just one or two but *three* astronauts flew safely to the moon and back.

Let's start at the beginning, though, as we all know and understand is the best approach to most any story. I'll start before the United States reached that point of actually sending an astronaut safely into the upper regions of space. The first manned spaceflight was launched by the good and proud people of the Soviet Union on April 12, 1961, with the cosmonaut Yuri Gagarin.

Just twenty-three days later the United States successfully sent its first astronaut into space. This well-documented event took place on May 5, 1961. Astronaut Alan Bartlett Shepard was the first American astronaut to reach outer space and successfully maintain a brief, controlled flight before returning safely back to earth. When telling any story like this one, for accuracy it's always good to include all the facts. So that's why it's good to remember that the Soviet Union was the first to safely send a man into outer space.

The first moon landing would take place eight years and a couple of months after Alan Shepard's maiden voyage into outer space. The entire world heard or read all about the accomplishments and setbacks of the US space program leading up to this historical event. Then on July 20, 1969, Neil Alden Armstrong became the first astronaut to walk on the dusty surface of Earth's orbiting moon. While doing so, he spoke the now-famous words "That's one small step for man, one giant leap for mankind!" It was a very powerful message indeed for all of us back here on earth. The impact of this accomplishment is felt even to this day.

Accompanying Neil Armstrong on this space mission was Edwin Eugene "Buzz" Aldrin Jr. Just moments after Neil Armstrong set foot on the moon, Buzz also stepped down, planting his own two feet firmly onto the moon's surface. Both men's foot impressions were left behind on the dusty moon surface as a reminder of their visit. While all this was being achieved, astronaut Michael Collins was maintaining a continuous set orbit high above the moon's surface in the *Apollo 11* spacecraft that had safely brought them to the moon.

But let me see here, were they actually the first men on the moon? And just how do I know the surface of the moon is dusty after all? Well, allow me to explain how I came to this.

In 1961, eight years and a few days prior to the momentous moon landing, the townspeople of Kodiak were happily preparing to celebrate all special holidays, and the Fourth of July was one of the biggest celebrations ever. This particular event was celebrated just as enthusiastically on Kodiak Island, as it is in any part of big city of the United States. Kodiak celebrated alright. It had a parade that included a marching band, followed by the local dignitaries, and then the other entries, which in this case included some ethnic dancers, as well as clowns, and certainly a profusion of other casual entries. As with all other parades of this kind, this parade procession included several local organizations and clubs, including the local Boy Scout and Girl Scout troops. The local equestrian group was the final act. It was smart to put the horse troupe last of the parade. After all, horses sometimes leave road apples and just about anywhere they want to.

All these different people who volunteered to be part of the 1961 Independence Day parade put a lot of thought and effort into their entries and how they were going to parade themselves down the short streets of the Kodiak fishing village in celebration of one of the most popular holidays in the Untied States. The highly dedicated organizers of the parade had encouraged everyone who might be interested in participating to come forward and register as a parade route participant. Without telling us, my mother had registered my two brothers and me as an entry to this up-coming Fourth of July Parade. This was the beginning to a very special time; my two older brothers and I would never forget how it felt to get all dressed up and parade ourselves down the streets in front of the towns onlookers.

Subsequently, over the years I have realized that most of these organized parades will change the theme of the parade while holding true to the old traditions, like including clowns, horseback riders with their decked-out clothes and polished saddles, dignitaries in brand-new shiny cars, and the local high school marching band dressed in matching uniforms and perhaps preceding those esteemed community figures.

Each year, in order to keep things new and up to date, organizers of these events encourage the participants to be creative while holding true to the theme. This parade had a theme all right, the long-standing theme of the Fourth of July, Independence Day.

Now apparently, for some time, perhaps for about a month or so before the parade was to take place, my mother, always a very creative person, had been busy covertly making costumes for my two older brothers and me for up-coming date with the streets of Kodiak. I have to admit right now that at first it was all sort of confusing to me when she first revealed our costumes to us. I saw her working on this idea of hers, but when she explained what the costumes were for, I had a hard time understanding just what we would actually be doing when we walked down the streets of Kodiak. Would it be the same as when we took our walks into town? That kind of walking or actually walking down the middle of the streets like I thought she said the first time? We would soon find out.

To begin with, my mother outfitted me in a pair of my oldest, most worn-out denim jeans that she had purposely dyed to a dull gray, a color to simulate, as best as possible, an authentic astronaut's space suit. Understand so far? I didn't at first. Anyway, after that was accomplished, she then took an empty cardboard oatmeal container and painted it shiny silver, completing the look by painting black stripes around the cylinder, just enough to give it that profoundly authentic appearance. Upon the completion of this simple project, my mother had managed to turn an ordinary empty oatmeal container into an authentic-looking reserve oxygen tank that would rest comfortably on my back. It looked realistic and functional, as did the astronaut suit I was soon to be wearing ... down the middle of main street . . . I remember what it was for. The way I was beginning to look at this costume, was that I was getting to dress up like have before on Halloween. My after-school play shoes, which were something more like a tennis shoe, were next to be subjected to the same treatment as my reserve oxygen tank. Everything was getting a good splash of that shiny silver paint. My astronaut space suit was starting to look pretty cool at this point, and like most kids that age, I couldn't resist the temptation of begging my mother to let me try it out. She only let me put it on two or three times, and only during the measuring stages as my mom took proper measurements so as to sow a nice costume for me. No other time was I allowed near it. That was probably a good idea too. It was really cool and kind of tempting after all. I mean I had an astronaut space suit—custom tailored—hanging up in my closet, and I couldn't wear it yet. Who else had their own space suit at home hanging up in the closet?

My space suit wasn't quite complete, though. I still needed one more thing, something every astronaut has to have: the ever-important space helmet. By taking some extra-strength aluminum foil—the kind used for cooking and making space helmets—my mother molded a crude but functional-looking space helmet, complete with a wraparound fixed microphone. It's important to understand that my mother was doing all of this at the time when space exploration was still in its infancy. She was basically relying on her imagination and what she may have seen in magazines. I point this out because I know for a fact that my mother did not indulge in reading science fiction books. Keeping in mind that a trip to the moon was still a long ways away, which made our moon-landing parade entry interesting and what was to be deemed "A novel entry." But what a great imagination; I'd say she did a really great job. Very prophetic as well.

Of course upon final completion of my space suit, my mother realized that I, the astronaut, would need some sort of highly visual communication device in order to explain to the parade spectators just exactly what I was doing dressed up like that. After-all, I was the "First Boy Astronaut to Land on the Moon" A simple little sign would do the job. The sign was very simple, but very important since space travel was a novel approach at the time. The words on this sign were large and bold so that everybody could see and read them. The sign would be the first declaration to the world—or at least to the world that I knew of, which consisted of only those people in attendance at the 1961 Kodiak Island Fourth of July parade—that I was the first boy astronaut to land on the moon.

Now every astronaut needs a spacecraft and that's a known fact. But just how to build a spacecraft, especially if it's going to be the first one ever built in a back bedroom and without blueprints? Well, once again utilizing her great creative ingenuity, my mother used a tall cardboard shipping box to craft a small spacecraft, complete with nose cone on top and rocket boosters on bottom. She fashioned the nose cone and the rocket boosters with construction paper and then gave this pseudo-spacecraft that authentic look by painting the outside with some of that leftover silver paint she seemed to have so much of. She highlighted the bottom portion of the cardboard box with construction paper painted red, which gave the appearance that the rocket boosters were blasting off. As I said, very prophetic of her and very cool for us kids. She cut a few vertical slits in the construction paper so that when the paper moved just right, it added to the affect as if the rockets were continuously firing. Though they were pseudo–rocket flames, they were still very cool looking, and from my perspective they were working just fine. Before my mother could call her homemade spacecraft complete and ready for the launchpad, she cut out a small area so that Fitzo, who was to be the rocket in this parade, would be able to view everything in front of him, allowing him to navigate the parade route.

Now last but not least was the moon. My mother's construction of a miniaturized moon was quite ingenious as well. I mean, just how does a person, the mother of three boys, make a moon? Big or small, it had to be a challenge. First it had to be small enough that it would fit going down the streets without bumping into things or knocking things over. Right? Plus it had to be something that Tim could easily slip into and yet see through since he was to be the moon in this entry. He also needed clear vision of what was up ahead in order to navigate the parade route, yet he had to be hidden enough that the parade spectators didn't concentrate their attention on the little boy inside the moon. After all, the moon isn't known to have a boy living there. The old-time fable says there's a man in the moon, not a little boy in the moon. Getting all discombobulated now. Well anyway, my mother went about making a small moon right there in our living room by completely wrapping a simple umbrella with some dark-green cloth. That was it; that was all there was to it. Of course it truly wasn't complete until she placed a small American flag right on top, right in the center of course. Throughout history explorers have mounted their countries' flags or standards upon arriving to a new land to identify their presence, an act of ownership. It's also a sign of complete accomplishment and that was exactly what my mother did.

The procession was mandated in this order. My brothers and I marched in the parade with me in my space suit leading the way and carrying the sign that read, "First Spacecraft and Astronaut to Land on the Moon." Walking down Main Street in the middle of the day wearing silver painted jeans wasn't so intimidating or scary at all, especially once all of the people along the parade route cheering us.

On the day of the actual parade, the staff members and parade organizers instructed us all on how to go through the parade route. It was simple for me; all I had to do was follow the clowns. As a matter of fact, some of those clowns' voices sounded familiar to me. I recognized some of those people as having day jobs around town. It made it that much more comforting to know that they knew us kids quite well too. Maybe I recognized some of these people as being from our church. At first it was a little confusing, making it all seem scary, but finally it settled into my sub conscience that hey, most kids that age are busy showing off in front of other people anyway, and not that I did it all the time, but yeah, Ive stepped out of the house in just my skivvies on a few occasions before, so what's the difference. It's like its this way, being in the parade in costume was the exact same thing as showing off in front of everyone around the house, only I was showing off in some kind of super-cool looking one of a kind costume no less. It's a memory I will always cherish and remember how much fun it was to walk down the streets of Kodiak holding up a sign explaining to everyone who could read, how the moon landing was not only possible, but I was the first boy to achieve this. Believe me, this was a whole lot more fun than I first thought it would be. I was immediately myself once again, just being a show-off. After all, remember now, we were following the clowns. This has turned out to be one of the best things I ever involved myself in as a kid.

Back to the order of responsibility. Now since I was the astronaut and was carrying the sign, I would be leading us three boys in our place among the other parade participants. Then again, I wasn't really leading, more like following. All the same, following behind me would be the spacecraft, disguising my brother Fitzo, that I, the astronaut here, would use in order to reach the moon. Bringing up our procession was our destination, the moon, concealing my brother Tim.

We walked behind the clowns down the street, turning onto an series of street which ultimately lead us to the end of the parade route where all the people would eventually end up and congregate in true form in celebration of the Fourth of July. How convenient that the daylong Fourth of July celebration just so happened to be at the same spot where just a couple of months earlier we were all celebrating the Kodiak Crab Festival. That was such a great time for me, as I'll always remember how we paraded down the parade route, with those many spectators lining the streets applauding us as we marched on by. My brothers and I were such a standout in the 1961 Fourth of July parade that the local newspaper, the *Kodiak Mirror*, mentioned our entry and our costumes the following day. Though our first names were omitted from this article, as well as my mothers name, the paper did call us a "novel entry in the parade." Remember, not for another eight years would Neil Armstrong first step foot on the moon.

Over the years, I've often recalled parading down the street in our costumes and the good times and great thoughts I gained all because of my mother's diligent efforts in putting those costumes together so that we kids could enjoy participating in this exciting event right along with others. Those are some of the best memories I have as a kid, and they always bring me an immediate smile.

Thanks a lot, Mom! You're great! Moms and Dads everywhere are great!

I'm Not Just Another
Screen-Door Witness

As the summer months continued on, so did my lessons in understanding the world in general. For me, getting out of the house every day in order to go explore something new was absolutely quintessential to being a happy child. Seriously, staying in the house on any day with tolerable weather outdoors was like house arrest to me. I was always ready for a family outing. Empowered by my family's encouragement, I just naturally took to the outdoors. Maybe it was from all those repetitive lessons regarding the wildlife and particularly about the bears. My brother Tim was the same way. The outdoors were truly intriguing with so very much to explore and witness firsthand.

One of our more-often-chosen outdoor summer activities was a nice, modestly prepared picnic out on one of the local littorals—a nice beach along the ocean waterfront or perhaps a nice sandy beach alongside one of the lakes or rivers that flowed nearby. Our choices for the perfect picnic spot on just about any day of the year were endless.

Our typical picnic basket for our weekday picnics consisted of basic comestibles, such as sliced fruit and cheese with some soda crackers—definitely sandy-beach-appropriate food. Those picnic baskets almost always included kid-favorite hot dogs. I remember how much fun we kids got out of roasting hot dogs over an open fire pit, on any particular beach no less. Somehow those hot dogs just tasted way better outdoors and roasted over an open fire. If there's going to be any kind of a picnic out on a coastal beaches, then hot dogs are truly an important go-to item for every properly prepared picnic menu—as far as a kid are concerned anyway. Open-pit, flame-roasted hot dogs on the beaches of Kodiak Island were the absolute best!

Of course we didn't have hot dogs on every picnic. Sometimes we would have hobo-style hot dogs, which are bologna slices rolled up like hot dogs. They were great too, but I never could roast them the way I could a regular hot dog. Believe me, we tried, and gave it an honest effort as only a curious child could do. I always favored the peanut-butter-and-jelly sandwich for outdoor picnics too, but I personally found out early on that sand has a way of getting into just about any sandwich. Beach sand in a peanut-butter-and-jelly sandwich is disgusting and quite frankly I won't have it. Sand on a hot dog, not such a big deal, but sand mixed with peanut butter, and there's just no spitting that out. Like with a hot dog, just spit it out and move on—no big surprise there. Besides, it's not like my hot dog didn't fall into the fire a few times while I was roasting it.

And to help wash it all down—"Belly-wash" is what my grandpa G would always say—we drank water. That was it, just water to drink. We rarely ever had anything else, and when we did, they were unsweetened flavored drinks, powder varieties mixed with water. Never did we get to drink anything else. Okay, we also drank milk and even chocolate milk sometimes, but us kids were denied of having soda. I eventually had my first taste of cola around the age of fourteen.

If my dad was coming along on the picnic too, well, we'd just bring along the bigger, more elaborate picnic basket. Plus we would feast on fried chicken and potato salad or maybe coleslaw and perhaps roast hot dogs. My dad loved hot dogs too of course, but precooked chicken was his favorite, and who could argue with that type of logic? Except maybe a diehard fan of open-pit, fire roasted hotdogs.

Another perk to living in this beautiful town was that within a twenty-minute drive in either direction, we could be at any number of secluded public beaches. Lizzie always seemed to be the easiest one to please in the gang. She had an any-beach-will-do attitude, and for us kids it really didn't matter which beach we visited either, since every beach had it's own unique attributes. Our decision about which beach to go to each time was pretty much based on what we wanted to explore and which beach had that particular potential. Practically any beach would suffice, and there were plenty of beaches to choose from, but sometimes we just wanted to roast hot dogs and explore, while other times we wanted to picnic, as well as go swimming. Swimming and running the length of the beachfront with Lizzie was pretty much all I did or could do on some of those beaches. Some beaches were perfect for when we went swimming, while some days we kids instead just wanted to explored the beaches, where this one particular beach was the final resting place for a derelict ship that had washed ashore. Ultimately we would chose which beach to have our picnic that day, buy what it was we kids were feeling like doing. So many decisions to choose from.

This one particular time during our adventurous beach-combing escapades, we happened across, or more stumbled across, this very old derelict metal-hull fishing vessel just lying on its side along the beach. That rusted-up, dilapidated fishing vessel certainly was enticing and just begging to be boarded. And while it certainly had an alluring appeal for us kids to explore it, my mother called us back from our momentary insanity and told us that under no circumstances were we to even get close to it, let alone step one foot on it! Though the allure of the once-mighty seagoing vessel was strong and enticing, my mother was equally emphatic about us kids not playing near it, with the emphasis and a quick little lesson on the dangers of open wounds or cuts and scrapes from rusty metal. Very dangerous and mortal to humans!

Now of course we had the rest of the beach to explore, and after our grace period after eating was over, we had the option to go swimming. Don't be surprised here, it might sound as if swimming in the Gulf Of Alaska would be a very cold experience, but honestly, it's really not as cold as one might imagine. It all depends on the time of year of course, Having lived my entire life along the Pacific Rim and having swum in several different locations of the Pacific Ocean, I could certainly attest that the waters along the shores of the Pacific Ocean are brisk indeed and very invigorating. A truly wonderful experience.

Of course the freshwater lakes farther inland were nice places to go visit for a summer swim, but generally speaking, if we weren't fishing one of those freshwater stream or river or even perhaps hiking some trail, then more than likely we'd be found along some coastal beach cooking hot dogs and just hanging out with each other.

Confession time: At that young age, I didn't really do any actual swimming in the Pacific Ocean or the Gulf of Alaska, not in the conventional manner anyway. I mostly splashed around as little kids will do, bobbing up and down like floating driftwood. I remember also being really good at dog-paddling back then, so I was certainly keeping up with Lizzie. We had our favorite little sandbar that ran parallel to the beach about twenty to thirty feet or so from shore at one of our favorite swimming spots.

It was always a challenge for me to competitively alongside my brothers to see who could swim out to the sandbar first. I was never the first one out to that sandbar, but that's because I was still dog paddling, and they had moved onto a far different style of swimming which gave them the upper hand. That, and the fact that my brothers were older and more experienced. I really enjoyed swimming, or dog paddling as everyone else referred to my particular swim style, clear out to that sandbar every time we went swimming there. Thought it was a real nice swimming spot, and very popular with the locals as it had a couple of nice wooden picnic tables as well, however, as with popular beaches, there was just one problem with this particular swimming spot. Flotsam. Lots and lots of flotsam in the form of floating driftwood. Small chips of driftwood floating by us, which we'd pretend to be flotsam, were more of a nuisance that interfered with our swimming than they were a hazard. The source of these countless small bits of bobbing driftwood would be the effect of theses small pieces getting caught in a weak but steady current that would carry them on past us kids as if in a procession of their own, causing us kids a little momentary havoc as we attempted to swim our way around, navigating these bothersome bits of bark.

It interesting to see how quick it took me, but other than that first week, I never again gave one thought about those monstrous sea creatures that I had been forewarned about in all those earlier stories. I guess it's because we never saw any of them. Out of sight, out of mind.

BEACHES ARE NOT ALL THE SAME

Some of the beaches we kids traversed had the type of sand that could easily be formed into sand castles which could keep me happily entertained for hours, while other beaches in other areas of the island had a beautiful black pebble-like sand that, in truth, did very little to hold the shape of a decent sand castle. I remember these beaches being relatively close to each other, separated by perhaps only a few miles or I should say, separated by a few beaches in-between.

Even though the beaches with the beautiful black pebbles weren't conducive to building sand castles, they did in fact have their own unique advantages. For instance, it was much easier to dig the perfect fire pit for our hot-dog roasting in this pebble sand. I know this for a fact, as before our picnic could start, we would first have to build a pit fire. Now part of my duties to help build a fire, and that meant we need to make a good pit first. I know this for a fact because I helped dig those fire pits before we set-out to gather up our kindling wood. It was all part of the experience and one I looked forward to as often as possible. I loved those beaches for a few reasons, which also included a really cool crunchy sound whenever I walked or ran across it. I felt and sounded sort of like walking across lightly packed snow, and at times, just walking up and down these beaches and listening to the crunchy sounds it made underfoot was almost more entertaining than anything else. It really was a lot of fun just to walk up and down these beaches and listen to the crunchy sounds that black sand made.

FYI, around the turn of the twentieth century, nearby volcanoes erupted, heaving and spewing volcanic rock and ash throughout the nearby region. This beautiful pebbly black sand is the result of those volcanic eruptions. The volcanoes have been occasionally spewing this rock and ash for thousands of years. The culprits are located just across the Shelikof Strait on the Alaska Peninsula in the Valley of Ten Thousand Smokes in Katmai National Park and Preserve. In this area on June 8, 1912, a volcano erupted with such force as to send its ash high in the air, pelting the entire surrounding area, including Kodiak Island, with a substantial amount of ash. Mount Katmai and the other subsequent smokers are under a continuous watchful eye and are considered to be active volcanoes.

A PENNY SAVED IS A PENNY EARNED

"A penny saved is a penny earned" was a standard street adage of the time. I sure do remember hearing that old chestnut on several occasions. The concept of money, or at least just how important and necessary money is, is one of the very first lessons young children pick up on, even without receiving any formal education about it. This type of schooling came to me by means of observing others—a kind of absorption of knowledge by way of observation, followed of course with the occasional verbal lesson if I were to ask any questions, like "Can I have that?" or "Could you buy me that, please? I used the magic word, *please.*" Even with the magic word, the answer would almost invariably be "No, child, you don't really need that right now." Of course my parents were almost always right. I just didn't want to admit it. Both my parents were quite steadfast to their game plan to closely watch our expenditures.

Watching our expenditures meant scrimping and saving, as my parents liked to call it. My perspective of this scrimp-and-save proclamation meant that I could no longer just ask for anything that I arbitrarily thought I wanted or needed. It wasn't like I went around all the time just asking for things for myself, but the idea of scrimping and saving made my parents' refusal to buy me anything more understandable. And so, as a family, we scrimped and saved.

As with everything else, on occasion my parents would remind us kids of this fact. They would recite like a record the all too-familiar "You don't need that, not really." My parents' favorite was "Don't you already have one of those?" Time after time, we kids would play right into those engaging questions, as if we might actually have a decent chance to successfully litigate the issue.

When it came to money matters, we weren't going hungry by any means. After all, my dad had a pretty decent, steady job working out at Cape Chiniak, and my mother was a wise shopper. Plus we always got good bargains on food every time we went shopping at the military base.

Being thrifty was just one of those tactics my parents instilled in us in order to help keep us kids grounded while actually saving some money. I learned from this lesson all right, and what I learned was that I often wanted things that were superfluous to my needs and that I also wasn't necessarily ready for what I was asking for or thought I needed at the time.

Both my parents were wise with their money, and it was because of how they managed their finances that we lived very well within our means. We did all right too. I certainly didn't understand it at the time, but I eventually I came around to realize that, wealthy or poor, it doesn't take a lot of money to eat well and eat right or to live well and live right. I mean, as I said before, we may not have had much in the way of possessions, but we did have a lot of imagination, and that was one of our greatest assets.

I really had no idea at the time just how truly fortunate and blessed I was to be so young and doing all those cool things on that island at any cost.

NOT BIG ENOUGH TO FISH ALASKAN RIVERS

Because we were living in an area where fishing was considered the norm, it would only make sense that there was always a lot of excitement around our house when we talked about fishing or boating. It's hard to describe, or even know how to put into words the overall feeling it is to share in something as exiting as fishing, only to say that any and all fishing related jargon in our family was real special, and a subject matter that all of us kids would eagerly pay attention to. Out on our first fishing excursion I realized I had no fishing pole to fish with, so basically my very first attempts at fishing, became more about seeing how my brothers drown lots of worms and bugs. It's because I didn't have my own fishing pole that I didn't join in with all the fun. Now from my perspective, what I had garnered that day, and during the next few fishing trips was basically learning alternate ways of drowning bugs, and what kid doesn't enjoy killing bugs? But there just had to be more to fishing for me than watching.

Try to imagine for a moment my feelings of being left out after my parents bought my two older brothers their very own fishing rods and reels and not one for me. As much as they tried to explain to me, I could not understand. How come I didn't get one? I wanted to fish too! Did I do something wrong? It turned out that it wasn't anything I'd done wrong but rather something that I had not achieved yet. The problem that I faced was entirely due to my size which is confusing to say the least, since I'm a kid and I'm suppose to be small. The obvious fact remained that I hadn't grown entirely big enough yet to handle a large fishing pole, especially if a large fish took my fishing attempt serious and bites my hook . . . what then? What would I be able to do if that happened.

My parents tried to explain to me that, just like all the other larger creatures that lived on this island, the fish in these rivers were enormous and powerful, and I would do well not to try fishing until I was a little bigger. Maybe like ten pounds heavier. My parents were afraid that I might be dragged into the raging river if I ever successfully hooked one of those monster fish; dragging me down for another kind of fish dinner. By telling me this, they inadvertently handed me my first real whopper of a fish story. In truth, though, all of the various salmon that swam those rivers in Alaska—sockeye, silver, king, and humpback—truly were, each and everyone of immense body size and strength capable of pulling me off my feet into the river at the very least.

By this reasoning and this reasoning alone did I understand. If nothing else, I was persuaded into being quite content at this point to just hang out and observe while my dad and two older brothers honed their fishing skills. I was very content for a while just to watch and learn from their efforts. For a short time being I was okay with this explanation, and satisfied and content actually, I mean, after all, I wasn't too keen on the idea of my becoming some fish's dinner. I was much more content with the normal order of things, like hearing my mother calling out, "Come to the table for dinner now, We're having fish for dinner tonight." Yeah that sounded much better, and so for a while it appeared that I was not going to have a fishing pole of my own, and probably not for a least another year or who knows maybe even longer, or at least until I put on a lot more weight. I suppose that was the standard conceptual thinking at the time anyway.

Any other time or place and it might have stayed that way, but we weren't living in just any other place; we were living on Kodiak Island, and people on Kodiak island get things done and done well for their community. In fact, I was about to learn a very big lesson, whereby that lesson was to realize that I didn't need to go fishing for the big ones to have a good time. When there are little boys or girls involved, we have to learn to make exceptions and improvise. I don't think my parents ever entertained the idea of me using a smaller, kid-friendly fishing pole. I certainly didn't.

Earlier I mentioned how nice and friendly everyone here on Kodiak was, and now I'll present another example to support this avowal. Because this example proves that it doesn't matter how old or seasoned a person is when it comes to helping out another person when the intent is to make someone happy. Helping others can happen at any age, and happy is timeless.

It all happened just like this. One morning during the summer months while we guys were preparing to go out fishing for the day, the little neighbor girl, who was about twelve years old at the time—much older than I was—noticed that we were packing the car and getting ready to go out for the day. She came over and inquired from us where it was that we were planning to go do our fishing for that particular day. This was not an unusual question, since she knew all the local rivers and streams very well herself and had personally fished these local rivers on many occasions herself. Apparently her family did a lot of fishing too and she truly was no novice.

After we gave her our yet-to-be-determined guess, we talked with her for a while when she discovered that I wasn't really going to do any actual fishing, not really fish, but just hangout due to my weight limitations. She must have asked me how I felt about it, though I truly have no memory of our conversation. I think she felt sorry for me though because I had no fishing gear of my own. She realized that even though I had no fishing pole of my own, I was ready in my heart to go fishing.

Much to my surprise, this little girl wasted no time in inviting me next door to her house to show me something I suppose, just the two of us. She said that she and I were going to make a fishing pole together, or at least that's what I thought she said. I had no clue what she was talking about, but true to her word, in no time at all she had fashioned a fishing pole complete with a kid-safe fishing hook as well. I'm sure at the time I had to have been a little incredulous of her offer and her hasty assembling of a fishing pole—in her family garage no less and she said she was making it for me. I had never before seen anyone make a fishing pole and quite honestly not many people have. Even I knew people *bought* things like fishing poles and all the other necessities that goes along with it in order to make for a successful fishing trip. And to think she was only twelve years old at the time, and right out of her family's garage too.

Honestly, I was as completely spellbound as I was dumbfounded, as I closely watched her fashion a fishing pole, all the while trying not to say a word so as not to disrupt her which might lead to a mistake. I didn't want any mistakes while my fishing pole was under construction. The material she needed to construct this fishing pole were out of simple materials found right there in her family's garage. At first glance it might look like she was being destructive as she broke apart one of her wooden kites, all the while doing so with accuracy and precision, which is to say it's as if she made fishing poles for a living. There were two or three different kites hanging on the walls of her family garage, as she definitely selected the one kite she was willing to sacrifice. While I was impressed with looking at the other kites, I believe I was more impressed by how this neighbor girl, who took an interest in my dilemma, was at that very moment working on constructing a fishing pole that had my name on it. I watched her with great interest as she gently removed the long, two-and-a-half-foot-long wooden center piece from this kite, taking special care not to damage the kite itself as though she might have some further plans for the rest of the pieces. I remember this part very well; she definitely had to have had more kites in that garage than I first thought. This little girl was definitely a master craftswoman . . . no doubt.

After working on it for just a little bit, she tied a five-foot-long piece of string to one end of what was now the rod of my fishing pole. At the free end of that string, she tied a paper clip, which she had previously bent just so slightly a bend of the outside loop of this paper clip to create a J shape similar to that of an authentic, professionally made fishhook. I would like to point out this was a safe, kid-friendly fishing pole because the hook wasn't sharp at all nor was it a real fishhook. Plus if any large fish was to bite on this fishing hook, the whole paper clip would completely bend over, the string would break in two, and the thin wooden stick would more than likely snap before I was dragged in. Solution! Problem solved! Let's go fishing!

In no time at all, no more than ten or fifteen minutes maximum, she had it finished. This nice, friendly, helpful, considerate twelve-year-old neighbor girl had just manufactured for me my very own fishing pole right there in here family's garage. My first fishing pole ever! Now that is what's called a fish story. On this one story is a true-life fishing story!

I can't remember this young girl's name, but the memory of her kindness has stayed with me. I have always wanted to thank her for her generosity and her influence on me. Thank you, little Kodiak Island neighbor girl, for your generosity, your time, and of course your sacrifice of your beloved kite for this little boy's first successful, and most memorable, fishing trip. *Thanks a lot!*

That day's fishing trip went like most any other fishing trip, except for this time I got to cast my fishing line. As fishermen, my two older brothers were fishing alongside the riverbanks that day where the water was more turbulent and off limits to me. Even though I had a fishing pole now, I was still only allowed in certain areas. My brother were slightly bigger and older too, so they were allowed to go farther off down or up stream to fish for the bigger fish. I, realizing my limitations, fished the shallower waters of the same river. I believe Buskin River, which was one of our favorite places to go just to hang out so far was also my first river fishing experiences. It really was a very nice place indeed and has left an indelible impression on me. I have very fond memories of that section of the river.

It didn't take long before I had found a nice little fishing hole that was far enough away from the fast-flowing current to be deemed safe for me to fish. The river had diverted some water and backed up just enough to form a small pool, a safe haven for the smaller fish to hang around while remaining safe from the much larger and hungrier predator fish. So there they were, these little fry fish, just hanging out in this shallow pool of water for their own safety. Without any hesitation on my part, I crept up slowly and quietly so as not to frighten them. This technique is very necessary for good fishermen of all ages; fish can't see well, but they can feel the vibrations of large land-roaming predators approaching. If they hear something walking up, they'll scatter and go hide, or at the very least they'll refuse to bite anything offered to them … paper clip or not.

Contrary to what some people might believe, fish are not that dumb. Maybe the ones found in somebody's fishbowl at home are, but the ones in the wild sure are smart and very cautious. The heightened sensitivity that fish have toward danger is due to the fact that fish are low on the food chain. In order to survive they must constantly be on the lookout for danger.

Patiently working my way into position, I slowly and methodically unraveled just enough of my fishing line so that when I eased my paper-clip hook, already prepared with salmon eggs as bait, into the water, it would submerge under the water right in front of the school of small fry without scaring them off. Remember now, this paper clip had no barb, and I had to be extra careful that the bait didn't fall off before it reached the area where the fish were hanging out. But I managed all right. After all, I had gotten this far, and I wasn't taking any chances. I gently lowered the tip of my fishing pole, allowing my hook with bait to dangle right in front of the little fish. Fishing is all about patience, and it's very important to make as few ripples in the water and the least amount of noise as possible, thereby not alarming any of the fish.

It didn't take long before one of those little fries slowly inched itself over to take a closer look at this bright, shiny red thing that had just suddenly dropped into view. The whole time this fish had been studying this tempting morsel, it had also moved into position to take a bite, and took a big bite he did. I had 'em. I had just caught my first fish ever! Just like that it's in the books, and what's more is that I went on to catch three more.

I believe it was because I was so methodical and patient, that I was able to sneak up and systematically pull those little fries right out of the water. That was such a blast! Again, it's like no word could ever explain that feeling. These fish of mine weren't much to brag about, being no bigger than three or four inches long, but I caught them all the same, and with my very own special fishing pole nonetheless. These little fish may not have had the size and weight to bend my fishing pole, but I still had to land 'em. I still had to pull 'em out of the water and string 'em. I suppose I didn't really catch them in the traditional way, since I wasn't using a traditional barbed hook, but since I had enticed them to nibble, then technically I still caught 'em.

This was my very own first-ever fish story and the one I remember as being the most important one.

I was becoming a young man and showing signs that I could help the family. Big step for me at five years old.

That very same week, my mother wrote a letter to all our family members living in the lower forty-eight states, sending them pictures of us and explaining our fishing excursion and how I had caught my very first fish out of the Buskin River with a kite stick and a bent paper clip. This letter got the preverbal ball rolling, because when my uncle Marshall and aunt Vivian, who lived in Santa Cruz, California, received their letter and had read of my fishing exploits, they wasted no time in sending me my very first, professionally made fishing pole.

I believe my uncle Marshall, who was an avid fisherman himself, was apparently unaware at that time of my parents' position and decision not to allow me to fish with a fishing pole until I had gained a few more healthy and quite necessary pounds. It was because of his love for fishing, he had, over a period of time, accumulated quite an extensive collection of various rods and reels. Also because of this love for fishing, I think he understood the inner workings of my mind at that time and just knew that it was important for me to have my own fishing rod and reel. Nobody wants to be left out of the fun, and even though I never felt left out, this made the whole entire thought of any up-coming future fishing trips that much more exciting.

Of course like any other person, I now could hardly wait for the next fishing trip so that I could show off in front of everyone by catching one of those bigger fish with my new fishing pole. It was so awesome to finally have my very own fishing pole, especially one that worked perfectly for my size and capable hands too. It was obviously smaller than everyone else's fishing rods, but that didn't bother me, and honestly never realized any kind diminutive causing impact on my imagination because of its size. Measuring just a foot in length longer than my first fishing pole, my new fishing pole was perfect for me, or anyone my height for that matter, and just the right size to handle the many fish I planned to soon be catching with it. Special note: Giving credit where credit is due, is the only honorable thing to do, and this case it is to point out that my first, "custom made" fishing pole, being only a foot shorter in length, was also built to accommodate a little person like I was at that time. Both of my fishing poles were definitely made for me, or for a smaller, shorter person like me anyway. Without a doubt, my fishing pole collection was better than anything I could have ever wanted or had gotten so far. To me, it was like … well, it was better than a pocket full of gold.

It really was the best!

ARCHIPELAGO ... SOUNDS GREEK TO ME

It was during these nearly everyday outdoor excursions that I learned a great deal more respect for the area's wildlife, and not just this area's wildlife. These daily lessons also included the occasional but timely local geography lesson, all the while building on our diction as well as adding to our vocabulary. Kodiak had several islands off it's shores which are counted as being part of the "Kodiak chain of islands." Of course the common descriptive term was soon replaced by a more etymological word. More harder to pronounce perhaps, possible taking me the rest of that entire hiking excursion to master this new Greek word. Say it with me . . . 'ar-ca- pel- la- go'. Oh sure, it's easier to say now, but back then I was tripping over the proper pronunciation of this new Greek word more than my clumsy feet negotiating the uneven hiking trail. Ultimately one word, as soon as I could master the use of it, would replace all the three other words that basically meant the same thing. Nonetheless, this difficult to pronounce word was now the common vernacular we used. *Archipelago means "group of islands."* Because of this style of broadening of my young mind, that before I turned seven, I would be referring to and utilizing several words from at least five different languages with complete understanding of their meaning. English is my first language, and early on I was exposed to some spoken French words from the family members as well as the German words that had been spoken around our house since the day I first heard sound. Prior to moving as well as while I had been living on Kodiak Island, I had been learning many aspects of life, while picking up on expressive words from other cultures. A few choice words at a time, and soon I too was speaking Alutiiq.

What I had previously learned up to this point, and took away with me, is that life is full of lessons, and can come from all directions and situations as well. Learning something like new words from different languages can in fact be practiced at any time, perhaps even while casually hiking along a trail. I learned some beautiful new Greek words and how after a little practice I too could speak all of these wonderful languages. Some everyday common words that us english-speaking people use are standard words from other languages. *Archipelago* is one of those words. The word *Archipelago* is but only one of the many words the english speaking world uses while conversing with each other, and is so commonly used in the everyday conversation, that we become complacent not realizing that in fact we all speak many great words of Greek origin. Many english words that we commonly use as a society, have originated from the respectable and dignified Greek language as well as other cultures. The extremely beautiful people of Greece and their wonderful culture has stood the tests of time, and to this very day people everywhere, benefit from the contributions of the Greek!

Over the course of the next few years, I would learn a great deal more about this particular geographical "area," to which we were now using the etymologically defined word "region," and in place of "chain of islands" we were now respectfully referencing the "archipelago." Daily lessons were of the fun variety, and especially with this beautiful island as a classroom, where being in the front row so to speak, gave me the opportunity to realize the advantages at a very young age, that come by that of having a fine balance with nature, having and showing a respectful rapport with its many wonderments, that includes the fragile ecosystem as the indigenous people have for thousands of years. These types of lesson are considered more of an empirical lesson than a verbal one, whereas common sense tell us this. I think it's proper at this time to point out that during these lessons, our vocabulary as well as our geographical knowledge was increasing everyday; as was my confidence.

With the stories of huge bears still fresh in my mind, as well as the abominable snow-monkey stories, it's easy to see why I would be on the lookout for the obvious signs. Without first having any understanding of the area, people would say it was frozen, wild, and dangerous. And in a sense, it truly was wild and dangerous, but frozen . . . not even close. I think this place has all the warm of home. That's exactly why many people came to the island in the first place. Albeit, for some people it was strictly for sport-fishing and hunting, while for others it was an industrial fishing hub. For many years, Kodiak Island has been recognized as a major hub in this region for being everything from wild and untamed, as well as being majestically harmonious. And for good reason.

MODERN TOWN

Modern Town USA . . . not exactly. The US Naval Station Kodiak, as it was called back then, meant that this place, in some perspectives, was quite up to date with everything modern, from traveling vacationers to routine shipments of much-needed cargo. Being Kodiak is a small island, it must be constantly resupplied in order to meet the islands commerce. All major civilian and commercial air traffic arrived and departed through this military outpost throughout the day, meeting the needs of many who require the services of this type of air transport.

The immediate region surrounding the town of Kodiak itself is located on the eastern portion of the island where it touches up with the Gulf of Alaska and is approximately five miles away from the military post. Also, in retrospect, I realize that Kodiak Island actually isn't that far away from the mainland of Alaska or outside civilization for that matter, so we never really that far out of touch all that time after all. It seems that throughout the year, many local people will travel the reasonably short distance by some means of smaller aircraft, not necessarily using the main commercial airstrip, or perhaps travel by boat, all in order to conduct their business on the Alaska Peninsula or at other ports of call in the immediate area. Looking for a picturesque postcard-type photograph is as easy as merely focusing a camera lens when navigating the Alaskan regions.

Kodiak Island itself is encompassed by several little islets with beautiful coves and beaches which certainly will add an awesome dose of breath taking ambiance. Some of these smaller islets while having individual island names, were all part of Kodiak Island archipelago and sharing the Kodiak Island moniker. It should also be understood that even though it appears on a map that Kodiak Island might be part of the Aleutian Islands, it is in fact not part of that particular chain of islands when referenced.

It's quite simple really. The Aleut tribal people are the inhabitants of the Aleutian Islands and parts of the coastal rim of the Alaska Peninsula heading north on up the coastline along the Bering Sea and surrounding region, while the Alutiiq tribal people are the inhabitants of Kodiak Island and its smaller islets as well as parts of the coastal areas of the Alaska Peninsula and lower coastal regions following along the Alaskan Pacific Rim heading east.

While trying to be funny or perhaps artistically creative, my mother would on several occasional described the overall shape of the entire state of Alaska as the profile of an elephant's head, with Kodiak Island representing the short tusks and the archipelago representing the elephant's long trunk. Personally, I thought it looked like the profile of the great white abominable snow monkey with a long pointy goatee. Or maybe not.

Still confused? Then it's time to get an atlas! Don't go through life guessing at what the rest of the world might look like.

So there it is; the Aleutian Islands got their name from the Aleut peoples who have inhabited, fished, hunted, and flourished alongside the Alutiiq peoples in this area of the world for nearly countless centuries, easily seven thousand years.

Respect the Locals

I consider it highly respectful to refer to people by their proper tribal identity or name. The term *Eskimo*—which refers to all people living in a vast region that includes Canada, Greenland, Iceland, parts of Russia, and Alaska—became popularized by the masses without consideration for the indigenous tribes. It is an antiquated word that, if I'm not mistaken, originally meant "those people who eat raw fish." The word was not intended to be disrespectful, however, some people including some of the Alaskan Natives do consider the term *Eskimo to sound more* derogatory than endearing. I believe they would much rather be referred to by their natural tribal names or native Alaskan. Therefore, as the use of *Eskimo* is ambiguous at best and offensive at worst, I have personally chosen to adopt the terms *Alaskan Native, North American Native, indigenous people which is way more respectful.* Or sometimes when I want to show off my knowledge of the region, I'll use a particular tribal name or the tribe's location, as in coastal, islander, and interior Native Alaskans. I prefer to identify the indigenous people of the lower forty-eight states, to whom I live amongst to this day as anything other than with respect and the use of their tribal names, or Native Americans.

To the best of my knowledge and with all due respect to all the indigenous Alaskan peoples, I have found that the following are the standard and commonly used names of the main tribes or lodges living within Alaska: the Inupiaq people of the upper north; the St. Lawrence Island Yupik people of the northwest coast; the Yup'ik/Cup'ik people of the west coast, with a rather extensive experience and occupancy of the interior as well; the Athabaskan or Dené people of the interior (*Athabaskan* is the anglicized name); the Aleut people of the Aleutian Islands and the western portion of the Alaska Peninsula; the Alutiiq people inhabiting Kodiak Island itself, as well as occupying about half of the southern coastal region of the Alaskan mainland; and the Eyak people, the Tlingit people, the Haida people, and the Tsimshian people of the Alaska Panhandle and the west Canadian coastal waterway. These are all respectable tribes of people with their own distinctive dialects as well as their own sets of idioms. Not Eskimos.

Too hard to pronounce these names at first, but with practice and effort, it can be done. Referring to these Native people as Native Alaskans or by their tribal names is much more respectful and a whole lot more appreciated by these proud people who desire no less. Besides, using their tribal names properly makes any conversation a great deal more intellectual sounding.

Here's a heads-up: many people like to be recognized for their nationalities, cultures, languages, and ... hello, the rightful recognition and proper usage of their names.

WHAT TO EXPECT ON KODIAK ISLAND

Although Kodiak Island is approximately sixty miles wide and one hundred miles long, it is still considered rather small when compared to many other inhabited islands around the world. However, Kodiak Island is the second-largest island of the United States, although being large in land mass, it ranks among the lowest in population.

Many famous and not-so-famous people alike have traveled to Kodiak Island to spend some of their leisure time, however I know of no famous people living in Kodiak. Certainly no celebrities, or at least not any while we lived there. Famous people as well as not so famous people, would come to Kodiak to fish, hike, and do some big-game hunting and stay for several day, but I don't remember having any famous neighbors; except that one guy who looked suspiciously just like Santa Claus. Yeah, we were close enough to the north pole I guess, because Santa lived somewhere around the area. I know I saw him on a few different occasions.

Many people who have never traveled to Alaska, especially the coastal regions and during the warmer months, will automatically assume that it must be too cold for any type of long term outdoor enjoyment. In truth, this region of Alaska is quite tolerable and nice during the summer months, in large part due to the *Pacific influence,* or *Pacific persuasion,* my favorite term for the warming effect caused by the Pacific Ocean. The Pacific Ocean influences that dominate the pressure system in this area are evident by its climate. Remember now, the entire southern portion of Kodiak Island faces the Pacific Ocean, and the eastern edge is buttoned up right next to the Gulf of Alaska. Also, Kodiak Island, as well as the Aleutian Islands and the coastal regions of the Alaska Peninsula, sit so far south in nautical relation to the mainland and the much-colder northern regions of Alaska that the weather in this particular region more tolerable. Cold in the winter time, yes; harsh, no, not like the interior and more-northern parts of Alaska. I would easily say that the strong-willed and ever enduring people living in and around the beautiful cities of Boston and Medford, Massachusetts, endure way harsher winter weather conditions as to that of Kodiak Island. I remember that part about this Kodiak Island.

Statistically speaking of course, during the coldest months of the northern hemisphere, around January, Kodiak Island experiences average daytime temperatures of 30 degrees Fahrenheit. This mean temperature is conditional and can change from day to day. Just in case it went unnoticed, 30 degrees Fahrenheit is only two degrees below the freezing point. Just as expected, the hottest months are around August, and temperatures will average around 55 degrees Fahrenheit. Of course these figures are averages, and therefore it can and does get much colder and likewise much warmer during those particular months. Case in point, in areas of Alaska, during the summer months of 2013, the daytime highs reached the high eighties for several consecutive days until the temperature subsided and returned to average. Oh where, oh where are all of the bears during all of this heat.

NO BUGS TO TORTURE

Most kids around the world love to kill bugs, and I quite frankly was no different. I remember I had numerous varieties of bugs to harass and torture when we lived back in California. Pill bugs, earwigs, houseflies, snails, the list goes on and on, and all were at my mercy. I took full advantage of being young and in control. Torturing bugs was fun.

However Kodiak Island had very little to offer in this regard. At first I was fairly disappointed when I was told that this perfect island paradise offered no entertainment value in the form of my instinctual desire to torture and destroy the insect kingdom. At the same time, I was also informed that there were no snakes to be found in Alaska either. That was great to hear. Sort of an even balance there: no bugs to torture yet no nasty snakes to be bothered with.

Over the years I've come to understand that in some countries and cultures, it's customary and widely considered gourmet dining to sample the various local edible bugs. Some areas of the world have large insects inhabiting their local fauna and flora, and the local people consume these bugs on a daily basis. In some cases the local bugs are eaten as an important dietary staple. Now I know for a fact that some French people, as well as people from other parts of the world, dine on escargot, or snails, and consider it to be rather enjoyable. Interesting to say the least, but that's not where I'm going with this. Not at all. And I'm not trying to entice others to go out and have bugs for dinner tonight.

It's like this, whether enjoying bugs for food or for mere torturous studies, Kodiak had zilch in the way of bugs that I was familiar with as a child who loved bugs for both observational entertainment purposes as well as for the childish torture.

Of course there are certain bugs that thrive in Alaska, just not the same type of bugs that I was used to messing with. Among those selective bugs in Alaska are mosquitoes. Bigger than big, nasty mosquitoes. Sadly, Alaska is notorious for having a large population of mosquitos, and for good reason too. After all, mosquitos are linked to water, and take full advantage of Alaska' many rivers and streams that constantly pooling up offering these ideal areas during their seasons. Ideal habitat for mosquitoes to breed and thrive. Probably the most frustrating thing to these nasty bugs was that It was impossible to torture mosquitos by pulling their wings off. Kids will be kids, and after a good smack, well there's just no fun in it anymore.

So when in Alaska, watch out for those pesky, ridiculously large mosquitoes. Watch out . . . *Incoming!*

FYI, someone who studies bugs is called an entomologist. Now a person who eats bugs is either called a survivalist, a true connoisseur of gourmet foods, or someone who's just flat-out hungry. Either way, it's all good. Chalk it up as just another cultural diversity. The first time I heard of people eating raw fish it didn't sound appealing to me either, until I tried it. The benefits of keeping it cool with other people, holding with reverence, their cultural differences and styles of traversing life are worth more than gold. An old maxim says, "Try it; you'll like it."

KINDERGARTEN

Whether you recognize and celebrate your annual birthday or not, the fact still remains that each and every year, just like clockwork, we all get one year older. This type of reality check is perfect for little kids and people young at heart because they very much enjoy birthday celebrations in the company of friends and family. Truth be told, one's birthday celebration is one of the best times of the year for many people, no matter how old they are.

For me, turning five years old was way better than my first four birthdays and for good reason—well because for one thing, I felt way more confident about myself for one thing, which can easily be credited to all my many great adventures that I had been participating in for the previous twelve months. Of course turning five years old is a big birthday moment for most kids because it's at this age that most kids begin to realize that they are getting a little older and will soon be attending school for the first time. I, for one, was rather excited about the whole prospect of going to school and couldn't wait to do so. An awesome feeling of accomplishment that cannot be described or expressed. The awesome feeling that I too would soon be a student just like my two older brothers. I was finally at that age where I qualified to receive the proper teachings in order to obtain a higher education. A time when . . . wait a minute here, it's just kindergarten.

Well now, just like clockwork, the end of summer was fast approaching, and as it has been customary, signaling the beginning of a brand-new school year and where everything is about to begin for me because now I was going to get to go to school like all the older kids do. By the time school started, it was all I could think about since after all, my brother Tim went to school the previous year and had told me all about it. Well, most of it I'm sure, since he couldn't really explain just exactly whatI was about to experience..

Now I have to say, my first day of kindergarten was sort of confusing truth be told, though I really can't remember much about the particulars of that first day any way. Meeting the kindergarten teacher for the first time that day was a little weird to me because the kindergarten teacher was a family friend Mrs. Cornelius. Sound familiar? Mr. and Mrs. G Cornelius and my parents were friends and also had a gold-prospecting stake together, and here along Mrs Cornelius was the kindergarten teacher as well. It sure is a small world, but was this the norm, I mean does Mr. Cornelius teach archeology? Honestly though, I had no idea what so ever that Mrs. Cornelius, the lady who had come over to our house with her husband on several prior visits to share dinner with was the kindergarten teacher.

On that first day as a kindergartener, I was able to recognize a few of the local kids who lived in my small neighborhood, though there were also kids whom I had never seen before. A lot more kids too. Those other kids must have lived in town or some other area far past my restrictive boundaries. It was amazing to me that this little town had so many other kids my own age whom I had no prior knowledge of. But there we all were, less than thirty young, eager pupils, all raring to get educated. And by the end of my first week of kindergarten, I had several new friends.

Being raised to be observant of my surroundings, I couldn't help but notice while walking home from school that some of my new classmates and friends lived fairly close to where I lived, and in truth, some of these kids lived just down the street from us, but on the other side of the imaginary boundary line that my parents had put in place for me in order to keep me from wandering. Apparently these kids had similar restrictions placed on them by their own parents as well.

Education begins with understanding, and before long all of us kindergarteners were finger painting and mastering the art of getting along with each other. Another introduction into one of life's many pleasures experienced at this age was learning how to use and master a dull pair of scissors. We were all taught to master this tool so by the time Thanksgiving, one of our most favorite holidays arrived, we would have created little cutouts and duplicate copies of our outlined hands on paper, and paste these cutouts onto another larger piece of paper. Strategically placing some brown and green and red water paint, I quickly transformed my hand cutout into a colorful little imitation turkey birds. Our teacher said we would be taking our artwork home for our parents to see our progress in our education, so she instructed us to do a good job, all the while convincing us that our parents would be extremely happy with our efforts. So I did the very best I could and I don't mind saying that my artwork turned out to be a masterpiece alright.

I'm sure I had to have been thinking at the time that if this was what they considered higher education, then I must be some sort of genius. I mean, look what I could do!

These particular pieces of refrigerator art, considered by some to be masterful craftsmanship, were always fun for me to create. In no time at all the refrigerator at our house was completely covered with amazing art. I'll say no more about this masterful artwork.

How great my parents were, to be so proud of my young creativity as to adorn the refrigerator and proudly display my creative efforts.

Ah yes, the beginnings of my higher education. Just look at me work the abacus now!

BLINK OF AN EYE

The school year only lasts for a short while, and in the blink of an eye, or nap in this case, kindergarten was over. It was springtime, and that meant school season was over for the summer—a three-month vacation. For the first time I now understand what it meant to have a summer break, to have the summer months all to myself away from school. Plus the next school year I was going to be in first grade so I was feeling pretty good. In essence, I was temporarily saying good-bye to my new friends and classmates for the summer hiatus, with the intention of coming back next fall to continue my schooling.

Unbeknownst to me at the time, I had entered into an age-old fraternity, had completed a rite of passage, so to speak, that all students experience. This ritual would continue for every school that I would attend. My brother Tim and I eventually attended eight different schools in our academic pursuits.

Now we spent the first few weeks of our summer break of 1962 as we had the previous summer, playing around the yard of our house with Lizzie, taking our daily walks into town to get the mail, and picnicking at our favorite beaches. But then, not too long after summer vacation started, just as many things were beginning to make more sense to me, my parents told us kids that we all had a decision to make as to whether we would be moving back to California. Was that even possible?

Sadly, this news would ultimately mean that our time on this beautiful, awesome island, exploring and fishing for salmon, was about to come to a close. One summer of fantastic fun just wasn't enough time for me. I'd had two winters of the most-fun winter sports I could ever ask for, and I was just getting good at it too. We'd have no more adventures with Lizzie on the beautiful black-pebbled beaches, no more adventurous outings of any kind on the Emerald Island.

It would turn out be the very last time any of us would ever see the very beautiful Kodiak Island ever again, save for in our home movies and still photographs.

A Pensive Person

Now on one hand, it certainly was exciting to think that we could be going to see our cousins, aunts, and uncles once again real soon. After all, we would be able to visit and share stories with each other as we had done in the past.

I was sort of excited about the idea of moving back, at first, because I too now had some exciting stories of my own to tell. I could tell everyone all about this unbelievable island and how I had spent nearly every day exploring new and fantastic places. I could give my observations of everything without prejudice and with a completely open mind to storytelling.

By moving back to California, I could clean up some misunderstandings for my uncles and tell them that there were no abominable snow monkeys in that area. At least not that I ever saw. I could also tell them that I had found out a much-easier-to-pronounce name for the abominable snowman: yeti. Way easier to pronounce.

Back to reality. One fateful day, our family had an important decision to make as to whether we would remain living on the island or move back to sunny California. I remember that day fairly well. My dad called a family meeting so we could mull it over and decide whether we would stay on the island or move back to California. He said something to the effect of "We have a chance to move back to California. Who wants to move back?"

Without any real deep thought to the matter, we kids all said, "Move back to California!" The idea of moving back to California where our extended family still lived was very enticing. After all, who wouldn't want to go back and get to visit with their loving family members? Only this time I could be telling them stories of the many wonders I had experienced. "Yeah, good idea ... Let's move back."

After all, moving back just had to be a good thing. Right?

But then, shortly after we'd made our quick decision, my mother explained in further detail that moving back to California would mean leaving this island for good. Whaaaat? I believe we all may have spoken up too soon. It happens. It was too late, though; the decision had already been voted on and accepted. Besides, this meeting was handled in a democratic fashion. That meant that majority ruled. Just like that, I had placed my vote with that typical childish, quick-to-act enthusiasm.

I can't say exactly when, but sometime shortly after the decision was made, I started experiencing a weird feeling of consternation, a type of melancholy I had never felt before. I didn't like the idea of moving away from Kodiak, and would soon find it that I wasn't alone in this feeling. My mother and my brother Tim were feeling the same way about leaving this island paradise. We really didn't want to leave. Wait, can I change my vote?

Our second opinions were revealing the truth, that we preferred the way we were living and wanted to continue living on Kodiak Island doing what we had been. We just didn't speak up soon enough, and when we did, the votes had been cast, and the tally had been taken— hastily, yes, but we had made our voices known. The vote had been democratic, giving each and every one of us our say in the matter, even if our decisions had been made in haste.

Therefore it was to be. We were going to make the move. I loved California, but I also loved Kodiak Island and its people.

Probably no one's heart was heavier with the news or our upcoming departure than that of my dear sweet mother. She had such a strong connection and unique bond with the beautiful Emerald Island and was just beginning to pass on all her knowledge and genuine love for the island to us kids. She really had done her best to encourage us kids to witness and be a part of this paradise while we lived there. And live we did.

For me, growing up around and learning all about the peaceful coastal-village lifestyle and interacting on occasion with the indigenous people who lived nearby was a true blessing. What a great place to grow up and learn from the wilds of nature, all while learning how important it is to respect everything and everyone everywhere.

In a way, this experience on Kodiak Island can be described as melodically in tune with all the human senses. That may sound silly, but I have so many great memories of Kodiak and what it meant to experience life there as a young child. The things I saw while I was out and about were amazing, and the different smells were so intense I can still remember their influence on me. Of course everything I touched while living on Kodiak Island just seemed to feel magical to me of course I was pretty new to the world myself. Maybe it was due to my age, but I think it has a lot to do with the things that were going on around me. The sounds of rushing water from a beautiful creek or river undoubtedly has forever left an indelible imprint on my soul, as will the lessons I learned. And to partake in the celebrations, ah, the beauty of it all, even if it was just for a short time.

Such a lifetime of experiences in so short a time.

It Takes a Village

It took me a little while, but eventually I got over the initial melancholia I had been feeling in lieu of our inevitable leave-taking with Kodiak, and moving back to sunny California didn't sound so daunting once I had been reassured by the comforting thought that Lizzie was going to come back to California with us, of course, and that I could bring my fishing pole collection as well as all my fishing stories, each one better than the next, did the idea leaving seem less difficult.

On top of all this, I was much older now with more experience, and capable of actually telling a story of my own from beginning to end. The idea was that now I would be the one telling my uncles my own fishing stories—stories of king crabs so big that they dwarfed most young kids and even some adults, and true-life stories of living in a small fishing village where everybody was friendly and helped anyone who needed help because it made proper sense, and that sharing time with each other creates friendships.

Kodiak was a place where we saw local fishing boats every day and sometimes witnessed a local Alutiiq fisherman paddling by in his homemade kayak always with a smile and a wave; a place where I learned to speak some foreign words, like my favorite word of the time, *mukluk*; a place where I swear that sometimes the Pacific Ocean breeze gently whiffed up against your face to remind you where you were and to appreciate where you are at. It was an ancient fishing village where beautifully crafted lodge poles stood high and proud, towering in the sky with their symbolic and colorful statements for all to see, while learning that this silent pole actually spoke volumes. It was a truly great and wonderful land with so much to offer anyone of any age who desired to mingle with the grandeur of nature and strong-willed people as I did.

Moving back to California would give me the opportunity to tell everyone the true story of how I got to see Santa Claus practically every day, only to find out later on that he was in truth an older gray-haired, gray-bearded Alutiiq elder. I could tell everyone what it felt like to live where extremely large bears roamed the distant forests and fished the many powerful rivers and streams teaming with salmon with little or no hyperbole, but told perhaps with a little childish bravado. I'll certainly have to tell everyone the stories about us picnicking the many different beaches and becoming readied beachcombers and sometimes taking a swim in the waters of the great Pacific Ocean and Gulf of Alaska. Definitely an indelible memory for all of us, with an equally indelible memory of our exposure to the Alutiiq people, their culture, learning some of their dialect and customs, including the cultural similarities we all share like the ever-loving and comforting readied smile, something these people were very good at.

In a short period of time, we had become invested citizens of a fairly small, yet diverse community on an island in the Gulf of Alaska, where nearly every person was willing to offer a smile just as quickly as they were to lend a helping hand. It felt so wonderful to live in this area where people always had each other's backs, making sure nothing crazy or wild could sneak up from behind them. That has always made sense to me. I've never questioned that kind of logic.

Now I could tell the story about how we lived in a fishing village as IDAs—indigenous, divergent auslanders. IDA is an acronym I came up with that identifies non-indigenous people who live and share an area for a long period of time alongside the indigenous people. The acronym is pronounced *idea*, and that is exactly what they are: people with long-term ideas of living peacefully in a certain part of the world.

After realizing all these potential stories I would be able to express the truth to everyone back home, all about the overwhelming melancholic feeling of leaving this place of wonderment because it was that warm of a place to live, and never once cold.

LEMONS TO LEMONADE

True to form, my parents had, as they had so many times before, formulated a very decent plan to counter this low bummed out feeling we seemed to be experiencing. In order to help take our minds off of the impending departure from our beloved Kodiak, they presented us with a diversionary tactic that would soon erase all of my doldrums completely. They told us that if everything went well, then on our way back to California, we would stop over in Seattle, Washington, and participated as fairgoers at the 1962 World's Fair.

Among the many different current affairs going on during that year, this World's Fair was one of the top things to do. The Seattle World's Fair had opened its doors to the public earlier in the spring of 1962, and it looked as if we were going to join in with the summer crowd, and take in all the action. This was all happening during a time in which the possibility of successfully going to the moon was still a distant dream, however the idea of space exploration was an enormously popular concept with the general public. Therefore, the theme for the 1962 World's Fair was "Century 21 Exposition," which was by the way, showcasing never seen before futuristic wonderments of Seattle's own, like the first of its kind Space Needle with the futuristic looking people mover transporting it's passengers around this "Expo" in elevated monorail system, while giving all to see, from a birds eye view no less.

The idea of going to a World's Fair certainly lifted everyone's spirits to a new high, with most of the conversations around the house focused on those of our impending stopover in beautiful Seattle with our visit to the space-themed World's Fair, dubbed "America's Space-Age World's Fair."

It seemed that all I had learned up to that point, regarding this simple, carefree life was about to be immensely added upon. For me, and the sudden impact of moving back to California via the Space Needle, was as if all of a sudden there was all this space-exploration talk going on and, well, Im just saying. Oh sure, a year earlier I had participated in the local Fourth of July parade as the first boy astronaut to land on the moon, but at the time I had no real understanding of the message I was carrying in my hand or what kind of message I was relaying to the parade spectators as I walked down the streets of Kodiak in my space suit, but now I was hearing retold stories of space dogs and astro-chimps and now it all started to make sense to me; I was the first boy astronaut to safely land on the moon. It was definitely a really great time to experience and participate in many great changes and moments in history.

One of the most popular topics at the time was outer-space movies. Many new movies coming out on the big screen and television were centered around space exploration. Those type of movies were showing up everywhere. Honestly though, I don't believe I had ever seen a movie regarding space exploration until we moved back to California, where we could get way better reception on all seven or eight channels.

Taking Off from Runway 1

Remembering back when we first arrived on Kodiak Island during the late summer of 1960, the only type of aircraft that could safely negotiate a proper takeoff and landing at this airfield were the smaller, more-agile propeller-type planes, and anything larger like those larger commercial jet airplanes were simply to big and cumbersome to land on this more reserved airstrip. Barring a dirigible of course, which would certainly have no problems negotiating this short airfield as well as perform a nice safe landing at Moffett Federal Airfield, back in good old Sunnyvale California, but we weren't traveling by airship this time either. Since we were heading back to the same city that we had lived prior to moving to Kodiak, it made complete, absolute sense that we would travel back the very same flight path, and particularly good sense since we were heading back to Seattle for a one or two day stopover. Time may change many things, but some things just cannot change, while the fact remained, this island's short landing strip had its limitations, and that's just the way it goes. Small steps at first to make big strides later, and in this case, from propellor planes to commercial jets.

I truly had forgotten just how big this world that we were moving back to was. Even so, for some inexplicable reason I was now eager to start the new adventure without any more concerns about it now, especially since I knew of Seattle, we had been there like almost two years earlier, except this time around, I'd be somewhat older, and had definitely been around the block—in more ways than one. I was, after all, a well-informed, seasoned traveler.

Before long we were all feeling a little excited about this new, yet slightly familiar adventure that was just ahead of us. Every adventure reveals a discovery, and though we had already been down this road before, or in this case it was a flight path, this was a whole new and different set of circumstances at a much different time.

And as with all due dates, our departure day had arrived, and it was time to actually board the plane and for now at least, leave this beautiful island I had truly grown to love and proudly call my home. I suppose that after our plane lifted off and we were high enough to see the island—no clouds this time—that I possibly looked out the plane's porthole window and said my last good-byes to my home on the island. Good-bye, Santa Claus.

As we flew off towards out next airport stopover, it's highly probable that I was thinking of our new place to live and at the same time hoping that our new home would have large, sandy beaches nearby where we could run and play with Lizzie just as we'd done so many different times on Kodiak Island. Of course, now being a qualified and seasoned young fishermen, our new place would have to have rivers and streams too.

Go to Kodiak Island sometime or anywhere in Alaska. It's not as easy to leave as one might would think.

SEATTLE WORLD'S FAIR 1962

I always loved it when my parents took us kids to participate in special events, and my parents had decided weeks in advance that, since we were going to be changing flights in Seattle, we should take a slight detour from our journey and take in the ambience of the World's Fair being hosted in wonderful Seattle. Talk about perfect timing. This Worlds' Fair was being hailed as the 'in' thing to do, which meant celebrities and dignitaries of all types were going to be there, even big-name movie stars.

Only twenty-two months earlier we had landed at the very same airport, only this time it didn't look all that familiar to me. I didn't exactly remember what Seattle looked like, but then that's the beauty of youth, everything seems a little different each time we see something. The very young are almost always amazed and easily captivated by practically everything they see, even when seeing it again for the umpteenth time it seems like. That can be said about almost any age, though. Case in point, most people go year after year to witness the annual Fourth of July fireworks display and the many yearly holiday parades. I would call that evidence of a routine nature, and though we see fireworks every year, we always find them fascinating with a renewed feeling of surprise. Now it just so happens that I have some personal experiences with these various types of celebrations, i.e. parades and celebrations. It wouldn't exactly be bragging if I were to say that I knew my way around a good parade route, as well as watching the fireworks exhibitions. The wonderful people of Kodiak Island faithfully observed traditional festivals, celebrations, and community gatherings as well as any community would prepare and host such an event, and people from other parts of the world came to partake and enjoy themselves at those events as well. While I had no real designs of what to expect, I had no idea that there would be as many people as there was those two days we were visiting. I was way more surprised by all the people I saw suddenly and all in one place. Huge amount of people in comparison to where I had just spent the past twenty-two months. Literally I can say that up to that date in time, I had never seen so many people at on place and that includes every international airport I had traveled through.

I have to point out that when we arrived at this Expo, I experienced a reality check and realized immediately, much to my surprise, that this World's Fair was a whole different story altogether in comparison to the amount of people that had gathered. The Seattle World's Fair had drawn people from all over the world, just as the Kodiak Crab Festival had, only many, many times more people. Many big-name hollywood people, famous singers, as well as people of all various avenues of acclaim to dignitaries of the scientific world, had all gathered to experience the thrill of and amazement that the 1962 Worlds Fair Century 21 Expo and it's motto "Living in the Space Age." All the while that we were there traipsing around the fair grounds and taking in all the action, a hollywood movie was being filmed somewhere near the area. I honestly had no idea during this time of our visit that we could potentially have run into someone famous.

Of all the surprises I had been witnessed to up to this point, this one single event certainly was the most incredible sight for me to be seeing, especially having come straight from an island fishing village, and now smack-dab in the middle of this huge international event. What the?! I mean … dang.

It seemed Seattle, with all its contemporary grandeur, had been preparing itself for the World's Fair for the past few years, busily updating parts of the city into the twenty-first century, with its newly built Space Needle and monorail system leaving no doubt as to what the theme of this World's Fair was all about.

People from all over the world had gathered in order to see and participate—or share—in the latest scientific inventions as well as world-class entertainment and food. There were endless varieties of enjoyable comestibles to accommodate the many varying degrees of taste buds and appetites, and while I can only speculate that there were many types of foods being offered, we kids were mostly focused on the corn dog aspect of fine dining.

I may not have completely old enough to have grasped the full impact of what was happening at the time, I mean I can say with certainty that everything there was so very cool to see like concept cars of the future, but were these the cars of like next years future? Things were just a little ambiguous to me at first. I mean personally I thought it was very cool to witness the monorail in action, and I'll never forget as we stretched our necks back in order to see the top of the Space Needle, but I still wasn't sure if things had changed that much in the world since we left Sunnyvale California.

It was during this time that the words *twenty-first century* started to make the general public think outside the box and realize that space exploration was now more than just mere conjecture. It was closer to actual reality than previously thought possible and almost everybody by this time seemed to embrace the idea of all this futuristic 21 century living and the endless possibilities.

The continuously ongoing breakthroughs in modern technology of that time were truly enticing and certainly encouraged many different people to conjure up ideas of their own spaceship designs, different futuristic styles of earthly transportation systems, and large communal-type domed communities, as well jet-packs for individual personalized transportation as well as many other far-out ideas.

John Fitzgerald Kennedy was the president of the United States during this time, and had recently announced on May 25, 1961, his positive and encouraging support for an American space-exploration effort. He prophetically announced to the whole world that the United States of America was indeed going to put an American astronaut and spacecraft on the moon within that decade of the 1960s. He would reiterate these ideas the following year in his race-for-space speech on

September 12, 1962, at Rice University in the beautiful city of Houston, Texas.

The type of excitement swirling throughout the modern world in the early 1960s was met with wild, futuristic fashions and some crazy-looking hairdos as well as with new and modernized housing. The 1962 Seattle Worlds Fair was boasting everything twenty-first century, with the likes of an all-electric kitchen no less. There were no private home microwaves on the market yet, however the promise of almost every newly built home would be built with a fully equipped electric kitchen as very few were at that time. Electric heaters were coming into vogue as well. No kidding. This was a time when plastic items were practically a novelty, and even the word *plastic* was rarely used in everyday circles.

The constant scuttlebutt of the time regarding newly discovered inventions, such as the microwave oven, and the constant discovery for the many uses of these simple inventions, i.e. plastic, as with the many new and fascinating everyday household conveniences were ever increasing popularity towards everything 21st century, which was a major contributing factor to the popular consensus why many people of that time thought citizens would be living on the moon or some planet like Mars before the end of the twentieth century. At times it even appeared that jet packs were going to be a standard means of transportation for most. Hey, by this time practically everyone was listening to music on portable transistor radios after all. I mean, come on, let's get twenty-first century already.

Colonizing other planets was a go-to topic, which conjured up many creative ideas, just as people nearly a hundred years earlier had been discussing the many possibilities of the newly discovered electricity or the newly discovered concept of the telephone. Before electricity had been introduced to the public there had been no immediate thought of the lightbulb, and up to that date, no such word had even existed. Then along with the discovery of stored electric energy came a whole new industry of nomenclature never conceived of or uttered before, as with everything new. The new conceptual of this 21st century, was of course was no different than the conceptual of the late eighteen hundreds regarding the new inventions of that time, other than the conversations of olden days certainly had shifted gears so to speak, whereby it was now space-age vernacular, which spread throughout the modern world like wildfire and was soon being spoken about everywhere.

Imagine for a minute, space travel was about to become a reality, bringing with it a whole new life-changing, community-changing, even world-changing concept, complete with a new form of words were being added to the everyday vernacular, a whole new form of phraseology.

I too had a fairly good imagination with limitations of course. My great imagination and willingness to be open-minded were probably due to all the traveling and education, as well as through my connection and close-up experience that my family and I had recently been involved in while living on Kodiak Island. I would be remiss if I were not to give a lot of the credit to my mother for helping to influence my mind in the proper direction for a good understanding of life's many adventures. Entering us kids in the Kodiak Fourth of July parade was just one of those great adventures. No doubt, I was the type of kid who was up for anything new, as long as it sounded fun. All this provocative futuristic talk had me feeling as if it was time to exchange my hiking stick for a first-class, honest-to-goodness phaser gun.

Yes indeed, the times were changing right before my eyes.

IT REALLY IS A SMALL WORLD

Now as I said earlier, a big-screen movie had been in production during this World's Fair, and while there were plenty of enthusiastic people from various industries present at this jubilation, none stood out or was talked about as much as the potential future living conditions and modern machinery.

Throughout Hollywood moviemaking history, there have been several movies revolving around state fairs, carnivals, festivals, and yes, World's Fairs, and all for good reason. One moviemaking company in particular was seizing the opportunity and making use of the already in place back drop. This movie production actually filmed while this event was in full swing. Using the 1962 Seattle World's Fair for its backdrop and scene location was a pretty smart thing to do—lots of extras in this movie, *It Happened at the World's Fair.*

The movie's main star was Elvis Presley, and during those years, Elvis Presley was as big a celebrity as anyone can possibly get. He was legendary for drawing in large crowds of fans, mostly girls. Elvis Presley truly was a highly gifted and talented singer, actor, and person of interest in many areas of the entertainment field, with a huge fan base ranging from the very young to the much older generation as well. Apparently we came quite close to seeing the very famous Elvis Presley and a very young Kurt Russell, who was not quite as famous at the time yet but still certainly one of my favorite actors of all time.

It was probably at this time that I started to realize just how small the world really can be. This moment in time certainly is right at the top of my list with the rest of the greatest highlights of my youthful experiences on Kodiak Island alright, just a different landscaping.

I was having some of the most incredible adventures of my life and all at this young age.

I May Be Forward, but I'm Back

All these many adventures I had just experienced in such a short time, and now we were arriving back to the Santa Clara Valley. As soon as we had arrived at our final destination, our new home to be more accurate, I got the surprise of all surprises at the sight of our new home to be. When we rolled up to our new home, I remember being confused at what my eyes were telling me. I recognized this house. No joke. Sure enough, somehow we were moving back into the same neighborhood and actually into the original rental house that we had lived in before we'd left for Kodiak Island two years earlier. How bizarre. Or at least I thought so at the time. I don't know why I was so confused by this, though I do remember thinking that for some reason it was highly unusual for us to be moving back into the same old house. It was nice, though confusing. It was like we went on a long vacation, and were just getting back, as I recognized some of the very same children we had come to know before we left for Kodiak, only a little older, playing in the streets as we pulled up to our new home. One big thing that had changed in this neighborhood while we were gone was that it had been annexed by Santa Clara, and was now no longer considered Sunnyvale, but now Santa Clara. Our previous street address numbers were different, but it had the same name of Agate Drive.

Of course this wasn't the biggest surprise of our return. I would soon come to realize that I was going to have to work around the house just as I had in Alaska, only with more chores now that I was older. After all, I was six years old now with some serious accomplishments already realized. Now before we had left for Kodiak Island, I was nearly four and a half years old and had no real household duties or responsibilities to speak of, but now it's a whole different story. It seems that while we were living in Alaska, my simple household chores were based on understanding that these responsibilities are common sense. While I was young, and given the chore of keeping Lizzie' water dish full, which I wasn't very good at but was learning the common sense of it all. I couldn't operate that cordless vacuum cleaner very well, but I had time to play, and when it came time, I was prepared, and by then knew at least how it worked. Things sure were different, yet they were the same for my parents, who were soon assigning me new responsibilities around the house. They called my new indoor responsibilities house chores and my outdoor duties yard work. They called these chores by the very same words as when we were in Alaska, only yard work in Santa Clara was a whole different kind of fun. Different title duties, same effort, and learning to have fun with the domestic chores.

It didn't take us too long after we settled into our familiar domicile, that I found a cow in my backyard. Its true, it turns out that my parents purchased a steer calf and brought it to our house, keeping it in our backyard for a short period of time. Practically from the very moment I first saw this young calf, that I then realized this yard work business was getting a little weird. The Santa Clara City health ordinance frowned on people having this kind or size of livestock in the city limits, so therefore, the calf was only in our backyard for four or five days, but, I have to point out that four or five days was long enough. Good thing too, I mean, what else can I say, but when a steer calf does his business step back ten feet? Maybe twenty feet is a better and safer distance. The very popular *Bonanza* and *Rawhide* TV series were very influential during those years, and having a baby bovine in the backyard was pretty cool because of that, but lets get real here, I mean what sort of an initiation is this; It's practically my first day on the job.

Well, let's just say that it was cool to have such an enormous pet living in our backyard, if for only a few days. What can I say, we were fun people, and once the word got out, the whole neighborhood showed up at one time or another, all wanting to take there turn at feeding him a small handful of hay or just to pet him. Cleanup duty for this animal was absolutely out of my league. I mean I wasn't any good with Lizzie, and this, I mean I couldn't even sneak up on it. I tried to get up close once, and help out with the removal, but the smell coming from that mess was obnoxious, and I was soon disoriented, or is that disillusioned, either way, I was no help in this cleanup brigade. Confidence and self-awareness where working over time here, as I quickly deduced that I would probably have ended up making more of a mess by trying to help clean up.

Now because the law forbids holding large animals like this calf for any long period of time, meant that my dad had a grace period of a few days before the calf absolutely had to go, which was almost as quick as it took us to name our new pet steer calf Blackie. We only had our calf in our backyard long enough to give my parents time to make arrangements for his safe transport to an eighty-eight-acre piece of fenced-in property up in the Clear Lake, California region where my grandpa and grandma G had been homesteading. It may have been only for a few days, but for a while there, us kids had the biggest pet in the entire neighborhood, a calf, look everyone we're cattle ranchers, if only for those few days. I mean seriously, who else has a steer calf in their backyard besides us?

At some point along the line, before we left Alaska to return to California perhaps, my parents had bought eighty-eight acres of land somewhere in Northern California, far away from the city in the heart of the country. The land was situated among the rolling hills just a few miles away from beautiful Clear Lake. This faraway country farmland was really only a couple of hundred miles north of where we were living in Santa Clara but seemed much farther to me of course. My parents had plans of having a little farming-and-ranching homestead in the beautiful bucolic Clearlake Oaks area near Clear Lake in where else but … wait for it … Lake County of course, where my grandparents would also reside while living out their retirement.

Keeping the little calf in our backyard, even for that short period of time, captivated us kids and encouraged our interest in understanding domestic farming to a whole different level. In other words, this steer calf helped to pique our interests in animal husbandry. Having a little backyard bovine for a pet will certainly do that. What was next? Goats?

OUR TWENTY-FIRST-CENTURY HOME

This time it took us less than a year's time before we were moving from our rental house on Agate Drive to a new location just a few miles down the road. Moving all our belongings to this new house didn't take much effort or time since our new home was located just a few miles down the road and still in Santa Clara city limits. This move to Santa Clara was more like a hop, skip, and jump in comparison to when we moved to Kodiak Island. It was definitely a far less dramatic event as well.

Actually, the phrase *far less dramatic* completely underscores the differences between the two previous times we had moved and this casual move just a mile or so away and by car only took us only fifteen minutes travel time to reach. This time our trifle little sojourn was going to be more permanent, since my parents were buying this house. That was a big difference in travel time compared to moving to Kodiak Island, however the sightseeing during this particular move was practically nil. Well, in retrospect, we did get to drive down the famous El Camino Real several times, as we managed to pass by a few of the last remaining fruit orchards. Included in this move to a new home was the promise of a brand-new house in a brand-new neighborhood with new kids my own age to develop new friendships with.

Our new home was located on the corner of Catalina Avenue and Live Oak with the very impressive, well-known Buchser High School just one block down the street and around the corner from our new home. I thought it was so cool to be living so close to a high school once again. This time we were even closer in walking distance to this high school than the one on Kodiak Island. Oh sure, I was too young to attend high school, since I was only entering into the second grade and all, but I was convinced that this was going to be my high school when I got older and ready for that type of higher education. And eventually I would get to attend Buchser High School, even if it was for only one school year. After my freshman year, we moved once again, but that is another story, one I'll have to share later. I will say this, though: after that move we did get those goats and many other types of farm animals, including turkeys, ducks, chickens, and guinea fowl. As I said, that's another adventure.

Now this new home that we had just moved into was just that: a newly built house. It had an all-electric kitchen with all the comforts of a brand new home. All-electric kitchen, hmm, sound familiar?

With this new home came a much bigger backyard and an even bigger front yard than our two previous homes' front yards combined. My dad took this opportunity to quickly educate us kids right off the bat about how we were all going to pitch in and help landscape our new home. The best news yet was that we were going to be responsible for keeping both yards clean and looking well groomed from that point on.

As we all prepared ourselves for our first day of landscaping, my dad took Tim and I to meet some garden helpers as he then introduced us to Mr. Hoe and Mr. Shovel along with a few of the other utility yard-grooming tools, like Mr. Rake and Mr. Garden Hose. We were told that these tools were here to help us and thats why we were to have respect for our tools. However, not one of these new Misters that Tim and I had just met that day actually did anything unless we got behind them and used them properly in our endeavors to upgrade and maintain the plants and soil around our new home. How convenient it was for us that the yard tools were there to help us.

Now before we ever got started on this landscaping project, my mom and dad had developed some clever ideas about what they wanted the front yard to look like. In other words, they had a plan.

With a few weeks of continuous, diligent efforts, the front yard became a beautiful landscape masterpiece that included many flowering bushes and strategically placed bushes and trees. From bottlebrush plants to seasonal flowering bulbs, all were planted with an expertise that I hadn't known existed in us. I suppose my parents were teaching us kids how beneficial teamwork really could be as well as to how much fun it is to work in the soil. As soon as we had most of the front-yard landscape project completed, we immediately started working on the backyard project.

Before we got too far along with the backyard landscaping duties, I began to notice the backyard was beginning to look more and more like the nursery rhyme "Old MacDonald Had a Farm." It didn't take long for me to realize that my parents were very comfortable with and knowledgeable around barnyard animals, even in city limits. As I mentioned before, both my parents had been raised with that homesteader-type knowledge, and they were quite willing to show us kids how to develop that same confidence and understanding. So there it was a well landscaped backyard complete with tow rabbit hutches, one beehive, a couple fruit trees with two ducks and two geese running loose around in the backyard. FYI: When keeping animals, always try to have a pair of each animal. It's highly important.

In a very short period of time we got to the point where we were raising rabbits, ducks, and geese in our little backyard farm. No more than a couple of ducks and geese at a time. It seemed we couldn't have too many critters in the backyard. After all, ducks and geese are very messy creatures, so two each of these fowl and that's enough. Its easy to imagine these messy ducks must have had strings tied between their feet and their butts because it seemed that every time they took a step forward, they'd poop. As I said, very messy backyard birds. Little duck puddles, gross. Oh, and we also had a small yet productive year-round garden in that already cramped backyard of ours. This had been my parents' plan from the beginning of our landscaping endeavors.

Now my outdoor chores included caring for our various farm animals, and while learning how to raise animals properly, my understanding of how to respect all creatures grew in regards for their practical purposes was brought into focus as well. I was now learning a valuable lesson on how to take care of animals for food purposes as well as understanding the compassion that we should have for these living creatures and there well being. By keeping these animals and by maintaining a good vegetable garden, we saved money on our food bill, which is the main objective of everyone planning a future. It worked out well for us too.

A Compilation of Lessons Learned

Alaska is a great land with so much to offer anyone of any age who desires to mingle with proud people and absorb the true grandeur of where beauty and rugged terrain meet. The five senses, unless compromised somehow, will truly come alive wherever we are. On many different occasions I have stopped what I've been doing just to reminisce about those days when we lived on Kodiak Island. I mean, after all, I still mind those same profound pieces of advice I learned as a child.

On many occasions I'll find myself doing something, and some particular incident might spark a thought and remind me all over again of what I learned in my formidable years and the fantastic time I had living in Alaska. I'll think of lessons learned by way of example from people who were adamant about forming and maintaining a really strong and great community for everyone to live in relative peace and harmony or lessons learned about how people, when faced with hardships in tough conditions, like the challenging conditions of Alaska, band together and focus on what it really takes to survive. These people showcase these lessons so their children instinctively know how to help a little neighbor kid with fishing-pole issues.

Camaraderie, coupled with laughter and a seemingly constant smile, can prove to be the best for anyone. The sort of friendships forged from lending a helping hand are the truest form of participating and sharing with each other. I hope that time and age will never rob me of my memories and perspective of what I learned as a little boy living in

Kodiak. I hope to never forget that gray-bearded Alutiiq gentleman I always affectionately referred to as Santa Claus.

Kodiak Island was perhaps a dangerous place to live all right, especially if you weren't careful, but it was also a very safe place to live, to learn, and to grow. My time living on that island was far too short, especially from a young boy's point of view, but that short period created a lifetime of really great memories. On the other hand, it was long enough for me and my family to have bonded with the locals, both the people and the wild nature. We were all certainly blessed to have had this opportunity in our lives, especially for me at such a young age.

Education comes to us in all forms, and the process of learning never really stops throughout our entire lives. In my early developmental stages of life, my elders helped me realize many different aspects about living a decent life. One of those aspects was that it's really not that hard to learn to accept others for who they are and to accept new challenges. It's rewarding even to attempt to do so.

NEVER GIVE UP

I leaned that If something doesn't seem to be working out, try to approach it from a different angle, and sometimes a time out really can reinvigorate. That's what I've learned through life. I've noticed that some things just don't run smoothly at first, and patience along with perseverance have gotten me through several situations. Sometimes I was too young or too lightweight to do certain things. The resolution to this personal quandary was not in solving my weight or age issues but in approaching my situation in baby steps. I learned that in due order many wonderful things will work out. We just have to be patient and wait awhile and then try it again. If those words sound familiar, it's because they are and because they work. Mothers and fathers all around the world echo these important words to their children, just as my own did. "Don't give up." Try to always remember in times of despair that patience is a virtue. It may sound cliché, but it is nonetheless the truth. Another useful, go-to adage that stands very true is "Good things come to those who wait." With all this knowledge, it would therefore be a complete and utter waste of time not to practice and live that good life that we were all taught as children by observation if by nothing else.

It is with an open and honest heart that I share these stories of my young life and the lessons I learned early on in my youth whereby giving some consideration for others. These life lessons helped shape me and mold me into the person I am today. Everybody living has his or her own personal first memories and lessons of life. I hope this book is enjoyed with the understanding that small children learn life's lessons as only children can, in both large and small understanding. Young children have no real language to work from other than what is placed before them on a continuous level. Children are born without true verbal skills, and what they pick up from their environment makes a big impact. Taking the time to gently talk to children in an articulate manner while explaining things will always reassure them—this works for just about anyone, but especially little children.

If we are to garner anything from life itself, I hope it's that we all understand the important needs of others, and this starts with our children. It's extremely important that we all stand together and also understand why it's so important to band together as a community. The whole world is one giant community, and we can and will always learn so much from others—from the highly seasoned elders with their sage advice to the very young and their own innocent yet wise understanding of things yet to be.

We should always remember to read as many books as time will allow us. There will certainly be no regrets ... no doubt. Try to have both an up-to-date dictionary and atlas in your possession. And remember, books are meant to be read and not just once.

At the next party you attend, notice which conversations contain knowledge and who exactly in the room possesses that knowledge. Everyone will have so much more to talk about after they're filled with truth and knowledge. It's a known fact that people find other people who are well informed and confident about their learned knowledge interesting and fascinating. Trust me; I know what I'm talking about because that's just how it works. Pick up a book or periodical and read it and then read another. Stay informed. This advise was told to me, I learned a great deal my keeping my eyes open, and hope some of this reminds us all about how valuable old school knowledge really is.

Here's my belated thank-you to all those people who helped me to understand life as a child. I know my thanks aren't necessary, since everyone who helps another does so out of concern for kindness, but thank you to all those people everywhere who are patient and understanding of the typical eager yet slow nature of children. Your patience can really help a child adjust much better to all the new and exciting things coming at them so fast and seemingly all at once. There are lots of confusing distractions for children. Both children and adults alike need some time to understand certain ideas or new and unusual sights.

This is not the end of my story by any means. It's merely time to move on to my next project. Perhaps I'll work on a story about what it was like living in the '60s, describing how the Santa Clara Valley—once known as the Valley of Heart's Delight and known for its wonderful abundance of fruits and vegetables—transformed its image as an agricultural valley and adopted the more prestigious, world-renowned moniker of Silicon Valley. Ever hear of it?

This current story of my childhood may be rather short indeed, but then again, just how does a person measure his or her childhood? How long do our childhood memories remain with us, and how long will we hold on to those lessons our parents taught us, hoping we were paying attention? In my case I've held on long enough to still exercise those precious lessons and pass those wise, old-school idioms on to others.

There really is no true end to our childhood. We get older, but the word *old* depends on one's own experiences and perception of time and lessons learned. We go through life like there is no tomorrow. We may look forward to tomorrow's promise, but we should always remember the truths of our lessons of the past.

There is no real end to our childhood stories … And this is not the end to this story; therefore, I will and can only say that that's that …

An Insightful Emphasis

After all we learn in life, at the end of the day, we all learn the most from our mistakes and others' mistakes. So therefore, I believe it makes complete sense that following someone's fortunes *and* misfortunes can be of great benefit to us all.

From the very beginning of life, I observed other people's mannerisms, which taught me how to speak and interact with others, and I began to focus on being talkative. At the same time I enjoyed the benefits of many people's kindness while learning to be kind to others. These two attributes of loquaciousness and kindness, among many others, came to me through my parents. My dad was talkative and gregarious, and my mother was kind to other people with the honesty and politeness that she had so much of. I certainly could have ignored their teachings, but I chose to adopt their betterments without argument. I have found throughout my life that other people must not have had parents who spent the time to teach them the essentials of life as my parents did for me, or perhaps their parents did teach them these helpful morals, and they just couldn't retain the lessons. I believe we all mimic each other—the good with the bad—from the start of our lives clear through to the end of our lives.

Having had no real contact with my grandparents on my dad's side, I have a limited understanding of how my dad was raised. I know that he started as a farm boy and was later caught up in a war of grandiose proportions as a young man. Having lost his biological father at the young age of eleven, he would most certainly have been influenced by the older men who served with him during the Second World War. His style and character surely must have been a mix of what he'd been taught by his family by the age of seventeen and the nurturing he'd received from the military and all its influences. Good or bad, it made him who he was.

I've always thought that it's rather impressive to have ancestors who came to this country from elsewhere, starting with my great-grandfather George, and maintained a love for their fellow countrymen and countrywomen. I've been taught to respect other countries, including those I know little or nothing about. We are all a community—one large community striving to understand with patience and being rewarded by our attempts at peace. We all make mistakes along the way.

Our elected officials are capable of accomplishing great things, but they too can make mistakes along the way. That is why we all need to work together. We have to always remember that we all make mistakes. Showing others disrespect because of their mistakes only adds to our own ignorance. And if we don't approve of what certain elected officials are doing, then we can vote to elect someone else. That's the beauty of democracy and the common sense of it all.

I was taught that it's perfectly okay to display my opinion, even if that meant not agreeing with another family member. At the same time, I was taught that there is no value in displaying contempt toward others and that it is never acceptable to throw a temper tantrum. Observe children's behavior, and you will understand better. Observe animals both in the wild and in domestic life, and you can learn a great deal. It's painfully clear that animals do not display tantrums, and children usually grow out of that childish behavior. Do unto others as you would have them do unto you.

Fifty years is a long time to watch and observe the transformation of others' growth. The world itself is constantly in a transitional state due to one reason or another. I'm very happy to have been around to witness so many great achievements of humanity and science. To give up on one's life during this transition is to give up on these events and the outcomes of the achievements. Live with the positive notions of life, and you will be positive; live in the negativity, and you're sure to be negative.

Live to share the stories of times gone past, which are sure to be cherished memories that can be enjoyed over and over again. Giving our time to others is a gift that can never be given back, and that's why sharing truthful stories of events that others were unable to be present for is one of the best blessings we can give to each other. *The truth!*

I'm very proud of my ancestors having hailed from Canada, England, Scotland, France, Germany, and Switzerland. I personally may not have ancestors that hailed from Greece, Italy, Africa, Latin America, Asia, or the Middle East, but I have close friends who do or who are even from those places themselves. I am so proud of my friendships with these people. I may not have ancestors that hail from all the many other parts of the world, but that's what makes us different. We should accept the innocent and guiltless seeking out of new territories to live, like all true IDA people. You see, living together isn't so hard when we all treat each other like a community, like our extended family.

We should socialize with people outside our immediate families with open hearts and smiles. Some people may not want to socialize due to the way they were raised or what they experienced through their lives. It always takes patience and understanding of others to get along. It's like that little Alutiiq boy trying to sell his prized king crab to anyone interested at the Kodiak Crab Festival. He overcame his apprehension of strangers in order to sell his catch and at the same time made new friends for life. Can you imagine his anxiety when he pulled this four-foot creature out of the cold waters of the great Pacific?

As I grew, I observed that every culture adds to the human race. Your footsteps in life really do matter to others, whether you know it or not. You can help someone and not even notice you did so. It really is all the little things you do for others that make your life big and full of rewards.

4th of July Parade Attire

August 1961

Underside of King Crab

References:

'Alaska's Kodiak Island' by George C. Ameigh, Jr. and Yule M. Chaffin
American Peoples Encyclopedia series
Webster's College Dictionary
Wikipedia
'The EveryGirls Guide to Life' and the 'EveryGirls Guide to Health and
Fitness' and the 'EveryGirls Cookbook' by Maria Menounos

Special Mention:

Raymond Newel Way- (dec.)
Nicole Cassie Way Hoffschneider and family
Alisa Erica Way Feith and family
Bill Bagnani and family- Best of friends
Keven Undergaro and family- Best of friends
Ken Presley (dec.) and the Presley family- Best of friends
Dave Roe (dec.) and Joanie Heinz & John & Karen- Best of friends
James Otis Moore 'Boomer' (dec.) and Rhonda- Best of friends
Gena and José Vasques with Iris, Lily, & Lainey- Best of friends
Tim and Christy Phillips and family- Best of friends
Joyce Boyd and family- Best of friends
William 'Bill' Haver- Best of friends
and all of my friends at LMSC composites 86-41 September 1978
to August 1983.
Dr. Steven Sheeran- Health maintenance and friend
Dr. Richard Fourzon- Chiropractor and friend
And to all of my family too many names to write, you know who you
are, and special mention to all those who help others thought this world
that may seem to go unnoticed.

Vocabulary Assistance:

abacus- used for calculating
advantageous- beneficial
amicable- without serious disagreement or rancor
anglicize- make English in form or character
angst- a feeling of persistent worry about something trivial
aphorism- a concise statement of a scientific principle
appropriate- suitable or proper in the circumstances
arduous- involving or requiring strenuous effort; difficult and tiring
articulate-express (an idea or feeling) fluently and coherently
ascertain- find (something) out for certain
aspect- a specific way in which something can be considered
atrocity- an extremely wicked or cruel act, typically one involving physical violence or injury
*auslander- foreigner; outlander
authentic- made or done in the traditional or original way

behave- conduct oneself in accordance with the accepted norms of a society or group

camaraderie- mutual trust and friendship among people who spend a lot of time together
cognizant- having knowledge or being aware of
communication- the successful conveying or sharing of ideas and feelings
comprehend- grasp mentally; understand
conceptual- of, relating to, or based on mental concepts
concourse- a large open area inside or in front of a public building, as in an airport or train station
congregate- gather into a crowd or mass
connoisseur- an expert judge in matters of taste
consternation- felling of anxiety or dismay; typically at something unexpected

convey- make (an idea, impression, or feeling) known or understandable to someone

crotchety- irritable

culture- the arts and other manifestations of human intellectual achievement regarded collectively

demonstrative- tending to show feeling, especially of affection, openly

derelict- a piece of property, especially a ship, abandoned by the owner and in poor condition

derogatory- showing a critical or disrespectful attitude

diction- the choice and use of words and phrases in speech or writing

dirigible- a dirigible airship

divergent- tending to be different or develop in different directions

eclectic- a person who derives ideas, style, or taste from a broad and diverse range of sources

elation- great happiness and exhilaration

equanimity- mental calmness, composure, and evenness of temper, especially in a difficult situation

etymologically- the origin of a word and the historical development of its meaning

familiarize- make (something) better known or more easily grasped

fascinating- extremely interesting

first-generation- designating the first of a generation to become a citizen in a new country

fraternity- a group of people sharing a common profession or interest

genealogy- a line of descent traced continuously from an ancestor

geography- the nature and relative arrangement of places and physical features

heed- pay attention to; take notice of

heritage- valued objects and qualities such as cultural traditions

hiatus- a pause or gap in a sequence, series, or process

hypothesis- a supposition or proposed explanation made on the basis of limited evidence

*imminent- likely to occur
indelible- not able to be forgotten or removed
indigenous- originating or occurring naturally in a particular place; native
infantile- of or occurring among babies or very young children
instill- gradually but firmly establish (an idea or attitude, especially a desirable one) in a person's mind
literal- realistic as opposed to abstractor impressionistic
*litigate- to dispute (a point, assertion, etc.)
littoral- of, relating to, or situated on the shore of the sea or a lake
loquacious- tending to talk a great deal; talkative

mannerism- a habitual gesture or way of speaking or behaving; idiosyncrasy
melancholy- a feeling of pensive sadness, typically with no obvious cause
mimicry- the action or art of imitating someone or something
mutter- say something in a low or barely audible voice, especially in dissatisfaction or irritation

naiveté- lack of experience, wisdom, or judgment
*nisus- a striving toward a particular goal or attainment; effort; impulse
nuance- a subtle difference in or shade of meaning, expression, or sound

observation- the ability to notice things, especially significant details
ominous- giving the impression that something bad or unpleasant is going to happen
outlander- a foreigner; a stranger

*participate- to take part or have a share, as with others
*participant- participating; sharing
pensive- engaged in, involving, or reflecting deep or serious thought
prate- talk foolishly or tediously about something

rancor- bitterness or resentfulness

tantrum- an uncontrolled outburst of anger and frustration, typically in a young child
*twaddle- to talk in a silly and tedious manner; prate

share- a part or portion of a larger amount that is divided among a number of people, or to which a number of people contribute

*supposition- assumption; hypothesis

validity- the quality of being logically or factually sound; soundness or cogency
verbal- relating to or in the form of words

yeti- a large hairy creature resembling a human or bear; said to live in the highest part of the Himalayas

* Webster's Dictionary